D0386699

PRAISE FOR JOHN EDWARD'S
ONE LAST TIME

"John Edward's story of life as a psychic communicator with spirits of the deceased is great reading for
anyone interested in the paranormal. I have witnessed John's performances myself, and they are
astonishing."
—Raymond Moody, Ph.D., M.D., author of *Life
after Life* and *Reunions*

"Brilliant . . . I recommend this book to anyone who
knows or needs to know that no one you love ever
dies."
—Patricia Romanowski, coauthor of *Love beyond
Life* and *We Don't Die*

"John Edward is a truly gifted medium. I've witnessed his remarkable psychic ability bring immense
comfort and hope to many, as will this inspiring
book. John Edward's important message will help
you here and hereafter . . ."
—Joel Martin, coauthor of *Love beyond Life*
and *We Don't Die*

"Mr. Edward methodically provides fact by fact
proof of life after life . . . We should embrace John
as someone from whom we can learn and take solace
in the fact that we do not have all the answers."
—Todd C. Pettengill, co-host of the nationally syn-
dicated *Scott and Todd* radio program

Most Berkley Books are available at special quantity discounts for bulk pur-
chases for sales promotions, premiums, fund-raising, or educational use. Special
books, or book excerpts, can also be created to fit specific needs.

For details, write: Special Markets: The Berkley Publishing Group, 375 Hudson
Street, New York, New York 10014.

ONE LAST TIME

A Psychic Medium Speaks to Those We Have Loved and Lost

JOHN EDWARD

BERKLEY BOOKS, NEW YORK

ONE LAST TIME

A Berkley Book
Published by The Berkley Publishing Group, a member of Penguin Putnam Inc.
375 Hudson Street, New York, New York 10014.

Copyright © 1998 by John J. Edward.

Book design by Lisa Stokes.
Cover design by Segal Design.

All rights reserved. This book, or parts thereof, may not be reproduced in any form without permission.

First edition: December 1998

The Penguin Putnam World Wide Web site address is http://www.penguinputnam.com

Library of Congress Cataloging-in-Publication Data

Edward, John
    One last time : a psychic medium speaks to those we have loved and lost /
John J. Edward. — 1st ed.
        p. cm.
    ISBN 0-425-16908-1 (hardcover)
    1. Edward, John   2. Mediums—United States—Biography.
I. Title.
BF1283.E34A3   1998
133.9'1'092—dc21   98-29707
    [B]   CIP

Printed in the United States of America

10   9   8   7   6   5   4   3   2

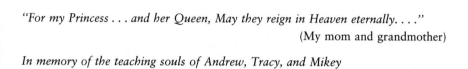

"For my Princess . . . and her Queen, May they reign in Heaven eternally. . . ."
(My mom and grandmother)

In memory of the teaching souls of Andrew, Tracy, and Mikey

C O N T E N T S

ACKNOWLEDGMENTS

I wish to thank everyone on the *Other Side* (and this one), family, and friends, for helping me to accomplish my goals and ultimately find the path my life was supposed to be on . . . If you are saying, "That's me," then you know who you are and I thank you.

A special "universal" thank you to my wife, Sandra, for all her love and support, and for believing in me and my work when I sometimes forgot to . . . I love you.

"The Boys": I have been conscious of my guides, a.k.a. The Boys, from the first reading with Lydia. They have supported, guided, protected, humbled, and most important, taught me most of my beliefs of the psychic world and the other side. Thank you all for making this possible.

"The Girls": Jolie and Roxie . . . the two teachers of what we are all here to learn about: Unconditional Love. I hope I continue to learn all they have to teach.

Mark Misiano: The BEST best friend one can ask for. Thanks for always being there for me in this lifetime, the last one, and hopefully any future ones. I wouldn't want to have one without you a part of it.

Lydia Clar: The reason this book "is" . . . Your words were, and still are, my guiding light.

Ellen Toomey: Your endless dedication to this cause makes you an ambassador to the Spirit World.

Joanne Woods: "The King of the Forest"—Your patience, compassion, and understanding is your gift.

Shelley Peck: Thank you for always being there. Only someone who shares in this work could understand the rewards, joys, and pains of being a medium.

Sandy Anastasi: The one and only "teacher" I had in developing my abilities . . . thank you for teaching me to be humble, and that it is okay to be wrong. Your guidance has been the foundation upon which I built and developed my abilities.

Ernie Santopatre: Thank you to a friend I didn't know I had, wanted, or needed. Your friendship and encouragement has meant the world to me.

Rick Korn: Thank you for helping to spread my wings and introducing me to "The World." Your energy has assisted me to teach the universal truth that life and love is eternal.

A special thank you to Scott Shannon, Naomi DiClemente, and my very good friend Todd Pettengill, of WPLJ Radio in NYC. Your friendship, belief, and support has enabled me to express my beliefs and demonstrate that we can all have a *One Last Time.*

Scott Robb and Robb Hollaway: Thank you for being part of a network for me to communicate my thoughts and beliefs. I will always have great memories of all our adventures in the FQ, RC, etc.

Tim and Michel Dahms, Lisa Kelechava: Your belief, persistence, and patience in my work proved to be an integral part of "my process" to help me teach "THE PROCESS." Although it wasn't always easy . . . I truly appreciate everything and wish to thank you all.

Buddy and Carol Dreimann: Or should I say, "Mr. U.S.A. and his best accomplishment" . . . You both have been great supporters of all my endeavors . . . and I thank you for being there. Buddy, our endless talks are like vitamins . . . feeding me energy and empowering me to be my personal best.

Thanks to my agent, Jane Dystel: your belief in me and this book has made it possible for people to believe in so much more.

Corinda Carford, Denise Silvestro, and Liz Perl: The Literary Angels at Penguin Putnam. I thank you for being supportive and enthusiastic about this work. May our collective energies be the catalyst for anyone who touches this book to be inspired to have their own *One Last Time . . .*

The following people I have met over the years and my experiences with them are like the penny in the pond . . . it ripples within me. Always . . . Thanks for playing the role of friend, and for being a part of it all. Steve Korn, Sheila Knies, Mindy Lang, Cecille Karlin, Ann DeMarco, Paula Monte, Ann Cerbone, Glenn Dove, Virginia (wherever you are . . .), Maria D'Andrea, Suzane Northrop, James Van Praagh, Pat Nikas-Lorenz, Fr. J. D., Sharyn Martino, Susan Blind, The Families of Andrew Miracolo, Tracy Farrell, and Mikey DiSabato. Rita Galchus Nunez, Sue Zummo, Rick Firstman, Jamie Talan, Suzette Cooksey, MaryJo McCabe, Victoria Lang, Stephen Reed, Steve Harper, Rose Tamborino, Ross Brittain, Kidd Kraddick, Bert Weiss, Bill Falk, Denise Flaim, Bo Griffin, Mark Mosely, Jennifer Valoppi, Mary Murphy, Meg Porter, Trish Arico, Neva Cheatwood, Joyce Coleman, Ramey Warren Black, Ken Dashow, Lee Speigel, Diana Ferrito, "Monkeyboy," John "Kato" Machay, "The Steve and Vicky Show" Josephine Ghirengelli, Judy Guggenheim, Patricia Romanowski, Pat Traymore, Joel Martin, Ina Rae Kurtzberg, Jackie Olderman, Clyde Corday, Patrick Lannon, Uma Pemmaraju, Martine Resta, Nina Resnick, Mary Roe, Stefan Ryback, Mark and Heidi Vandenbrouck, Arlene Francis, Del MacClarran, Paula McClure, Tommy and Joe Johnson, Randy Miller, Dave DiMarco, Grace "neg" Rivera, CD Travelplanners, Shala Mattingly, J. Glynn King and Brigitte, Raja, Wendy Wentworth, Mary Gregory, Larry King, Sylvia Browne, Viginia Rose Centrillo, Bob Cecilio, Patricia Collins, Phyllis Signorello, Anabel Maresca, Terri Stryker, Bonnie Peters, Claudia Raso, Donna and Tommy Sirianni, Patti Houseman, Kathy Barnaby, Donna Duisin, Judy Collier, Suzanne "Dale" West, Dr. Raymond and Cheryl Moody, Debbie Swift, Jennifer King, David Winkler, Dina Gehringer, Mike Sullivan, Bob Swift, Mary Alice, Planet Earth Books, Joel and Marlene Peters, Starchild Books, Joanna Langfeld, Victoria Regan, Tara Hamilton, Anita Scipio, Stacey Sullivan, Valerie Rummo, Diana Merkel, Janine Velotti, Steve Gudat, and of course Michael Wentink.

W hen I was about four years old, I
began getting up in the middle of
the night and moving around the darkened
house while everyone else was asleep. You
might call it sleepwalking, but I wasn't
walking so much as floating. Or rather, my
mind was floating. You might call it "mind-
walking."

I think now that I was astrotraveling—
having out-of-body experiences. I did this
night after night until I was seven or so. And
like many other things that happened to me
when I was young, I thought it was something everyone did, so I never paid too much
attention to it. When I began to realize *not*
everyone had these experiences, I decided
the thing to do was to keep them to myself.

One Friday night—I know it was a Friday because there was pizza, and pizza was
a Friday thing in my house—I was lying on
the couch in the living room watching TV,
when I suddenly found myself outside the
house. I was looking up at the window,

wondering, *How'd I get here?* The next thing I knew, I was back inside, back on the couch. I looked at my mother and father with what must have been quite a strange and bewildered expression.

"What's the matter, Johnny?" my mother asked.

"Nothing," I said, trying to hide my fear and confusion.

"You want some ice cream?"

"Yeah," I said absently. I decided I'd fallen asleep and had a dream. Yeah, that was it—a dream. But I knew it wasn't a dream. I was on the couch, then I was outside, then I was back inside on the couch again. You can't fall asleep that fast. I think many people have these out-of-body experiences but they do what I did—ignore them, block them out and say they didn't happen. Only years later would I realize that for me, these episodes were awakenings. Little by little, I was being introduced to what I would come to know as the spirit world.

Today, I am a full-time psychic medium. I reach out to those who have passed on to the other side, and reconnect them with the loved ones they left behind. Yes—to put it in plain terms—I speak to the dead. Or more accurately, they speak to me.

This book is a chronicle of my life and work, a diary of sorts that I intend to be a window into the spirit world and the fascinating realm of after-death communication. There are many messages I hope to impart: messages of love and healing, messages about the continuous nature of life, whether on the physical or spiritual planes. I do hope readers will find the experiences I write about in these pages as powerful and illuminating as I did when I experienced them. But what this book **is not** is any kind of final word on the nature of life and death and the dimension in between. It is a recounting of my experiences and of what I think they might mean.

In the years that I have been on this journey into a world we cannot see or touch, only feel, I have surely learned a lot. But I have not learned it all. Not even close. Many people ask me what it's like *over there*. My answer is that I don't know. I don't live there; I live here. I do know what I believe based on my own experiences, which include glimpses of life on the other side given to me by those who *do* live there. But they are only glimpses. I share them here in the hope that they will provide you with the foundation for your own exploration.

Although the true nature of the spirit world is elusive, what is plain to me is the spirits' ability to break through the void to let us know they are alive and well, and they are with us. The proof is in the visits and messages I receive every day of my life, messages I convey with the hope that they will bring peace and reassurance to the people I meet through my work. This book is an attempt to reach an even larger number of people by putting between covers my most compelling encounters with the spirit world, and to demystify this work by explaining not only what it is, but what it isn't.

The best way to tell my story and share what I have learned is to write not only about myself but also about some of the people who have come to me for psychic readings over the years. Every one of the stories you are about to read is true. They are based not only on my own recollections, but also on those of numerous people who have been kind enough to elaborate on their experiences so that I could include them in the book. In this way, what you are about to read is different from other books that have been written on this subject, whether by or about mediums. This book is about more than me and my spiritual beliefs. It is about the spirits themselves and the loved ones who have reconnected with them through me. These are *their* stories.

In most cases, I knew only pieces of these stories as they were happening. But through later interviews, I was able to reconstruct what happened before, during, and after our encounters. Some made detailed notes of their readings with me; others had committed the high points to memory. In a number of other cases, readings were tape recorded.

Everyone in the book is a real person with a verifiable experience. Most have been gracious enough to allow me to use their actual names. A few others, however, have requested that I use first names only to protect their privacy. Consequently, when someone is identified by both first and last name, the reader can know that this is his or her real name.

In all cases, I have tried to render an accurate and objective portrayal of my life in the world of spirit communication, without embellishment or exaggeration.

PART I

ON THE PATH

"When did you realize you could do this?" That's the question every medium is asked first and most often. "When did you first know you had the ability to straddle the physical and spiritual worlds and actually make contact with the dead?"

For me, there are really two answers. If I view it through the eyes of the child that I was, I would say I was clueless until I was a teenager. But if I view it in restrospect, I would say that on some very deep level I had an inkling at a much earlier age. Maybe I didn't recognize them for what they were, but the signs were there. Subconsciously, I knew something was up. I just didn't know what it was.

As a child I was always drawn to television shows featuring characters with amazing abilities and special otherworldly powers: *The Six Million Dollar Man* ... *The Bionic Woman* ... *Wonder Woman* ... *Spider-Man* ... *Bewitched.* I was ob-

1

sessed with *I Dream of Jeannie*. An uncle of mine bought me a bottle like the one in the show. Smoke came out when you rubbed it. In my mind I was living in that bottle. I imagined I had those powers—blink and make things happen. Was it that on some level I identified with otherwise ordinary people with extraordinary gifts? Was it my spirit guides preparing me for something I would not understand for many years? Impossible to say. All I know is that I was very specific in my taste in superheroes.

Not that I really believed I had any powers of my own, or that I was anything but an ordinary kid living an ordinary life. Until I was 11, I lived in an apartment in a section of the New York City borough of Queens called Glen Oaks. Both my parents commuted to their jobs in Manhattan—my father was a cop, my mother an executive secretary. They separated when I was in the sixth grade, and I moved with my mother to my grandmother's house in Glen Cove, Long Island. My mother's side of the family was the one I always identified with—the Italian side, all open arms and loud parties and family, family, family.

I was an only child, but it never felt that way, especially when my mother's younger sister and her husband moved in with their new son, James. We had three generations living in the same house, and on weekends there would be an invasion of aunts and uncles and cousins, all coming to Grandma's house—the hub. My grandmother, Josephine Esposito, had eleven children. So I never felt like I had one mother; I had six. Besides my mother and grandmother, there was Aunt Anna, Aunt Rachel, Aunt Theresa, Aunt Roseann. And cousins too, looking after me like big brothers and sisters. I think growing up in such a large and close-knit family was another preparation for my life. I came to appreciate those closest to me, to understand how important they are. Knowing firsthand how badly it hurts when you lose someone close has helped me do what I do. We all yearn to know that when our loved ones go, they're not gone. They've crossed over, and they're safe. I know how important this is because I have been there. I have yearned for this too.

One member of my family who had a major impact on me was

my uncle Joey, my mother's younger brother. He was a '60s-type guy who was always taking me hiking or to the beach, teaching me the value of the earth and the universe, and opening me up at an early age to the idea of psychic energy. He meditated, did yoga, took seaweed baths—a free spirit unlike anyone else in the family. I would watch him meditate, and he would explain what he was doing. When I was young, I would laugh and think he was a nut, but now I realize that he taught me how to have an open mind, how to imagine a world beyond what we can see and touch, how to believe that anything is possible, and to appreciate life, energy, God. He never talked down to me. And I think he was placed in my life for a reason.

Joey's second wife, Debbie, was a card reader. She'd read for everyone in the family, and I'd watch her and ask her what she was doing. "I get feelings from the cards," she'd explain. "It's like they talk to me." I'd look at her and say, "Okaaay." I was open, but not that open. Even though by the time I was ten, I had been having my own weird experiences for several years, I just didn't connect them with so-called "psychic phenomena." When you're young, everything you know is fragmented. It takes a while to put it all together.

There were times when I knew things I shouldn't have known. Simple things, like who was coming over, or who was on the phone. I knew about family history nobody told me about. I would talk about some family situation, and my relatives would say I couldn't know that because I wasn't around then. And I would argue with them. "Yes, I remember being there," I would say.

I have since thought about what that could have been. For instance, I could have been tuning in to the energy they were talking about and been shown pictures of the past by my spirit guides. But from an early age I also had the sense of having had a prior life, of having done things "before I came down here," as I used to put it. If someone asked me what I wanted to be when I grew up and happened to mention college, I would tell them, "I've already been to college." It became a running joke in my family: Oh, Johnny's already been to college. Before he "came down here."

I knew how to get places I'd never been to. And I could see words.

Even before I could read, I would see words in my head and spell them out. My father thought this was terrific, and he would show me off to people—the little spelling whiz. One day, he started giving me words: mahogany, machine, lawyer . . . and I'd spell them. And then I spelled the word *phlegm*. And he said, "What?" Phlegm wasn't on the spelling list. I'd never even heard the word, let alone known that it was one of those words that seem to be spelled wrong on purpose. I just saw the word in my head and spelled it out.

I saw auras around my elementary school teachers. I would sit in class and see colors happening around them. I once told a teacher, "You're blue." She looked at me and said, "Excuse me?" I said, "You've got blue all around you." She asked, "What do you mean?" I said, "Especially on this side. You've got blue around you." I've been told that I was doing this as early as five.

One day I was in Macys department store with my mother and said to her out of nowhere, "We've got to go home now." My mother said she wasn't finished shopping. "We've gotta go home right now," I insisted. "Phyllis is going to call. She's waiting on a corner. We've gotta go!" My mother gave me one of those exasperated-mom looks. Phyllis, my older cousin, lived in Florida. "What is it, you have to go to the bathroom?" my mother asked. I had big problems with public restrooms. "No!" I said. "Phyllis is waiting for us. She's calling." In my head I saw Phyllis calling us from a phone booth on a corner near our house. My mother rolled her eyes and took me home to go to the bathroom. We got inside, and within five minutes the phone rang. It was Phyllis, calling from a block away. She was up from Florida, a surprise visit. But we had moved and she didn't have our new address. Could we come pick her up? I thought this was a normal thing. Whatever my mother's private reaction, she didn't make a big deal out of it.

Another time, I came home from school for lunch and asked my grandmother, "Where's Uncle Joey?" My grandmother said, "In Pennsylvania. Where else would he be?" I said, "No, he's here, he's here." And I actually went looking from room to room, thinking he was hiding. "Johnny, I think you're cracking up," my grandmother said, laughing as she made macaroni. With that, my uncle walked in the door. I thought my grandmother was going to drop to the floor.

What was the source of these whispers? I had no clue. Nor did I have much interest in thinking too much about it. At night I'd go back to my dreams and fly around, down the stairs, out the door and over my neighborhood, everything below me a blur.

MAKE SURE JOHNNY'S NOT HOME

Y ou'd think that with all these strange experiences, I'd have been more interested in my mother's hobby. She was a psychic junkie. I thought she was looney.

My mother was constantly getting readings from psychics, reporting back to Uncle Joey and Grandma when she had a "good one." I didn't believe any of it. "Ma, what are you doing?" I'd say repeatedly by the time I reached my early teens. "Are you nuts? You're paying good money to these people to tell you a story." And she'd say to me, "Mind your own business. I like it. It's like going to a cheap psychiatrist."

Sometimes my mother brought psychics to the house for what I later learned was known in the trade as a house party. There was one, a short, old, and very feisty woman we knew only as Reverend Craig who did a séance that went on all night. Of course, I wasn't allowed to stay. She looked at me and said, "You, outta here! You'll have

2

enough time for this later." You can consider that either irony—or prescience.

Once a year my mother would bring in a psychic and invite people over for coffee and cake. One by one they'd go into the room with the psychic. My father would tell my mother, "Make sure Johnny's not home. I don't want him around that stuff." And one of my cousins would come pick me up and take me out for the day. My father thought it was nonsense, and I think it scared him. But as I got older my mother would let me stay. "Listen, don't tell your father we're doing this," she'd say. But I was with my father on this one: I thought it was just nutty, despite my childhood infatuation with TV characters with special abilities. That was TV. This was real life. And psychic stuff struck me as some sort of guessing game. You couldn't see it. You couldn't touch it. Yet, there was always a part of me that was intrigued by it.

Everything began to change around my fifteenth birthday, triggered by a scary incident. At my school physical that year, the doctor found my thyroid levels off and sent me to an endocrinologist for further tests. My cousin Roseann took me to the appointment. The specialist feared I might have a tumor, and Roseann called my mother at work with the news. Seeing how shaken she was, a colleague said to my mother, "I don't know if you believe in psychics, but there's one who works upstairs. She doesn't like people to know about it, but I can see if she'll see you." Lydia Clar said yes, and my mother went. I told you she was a psychic junkie.

It turned out I didn't have a tumor. But considering what it led to, in hindsight I've come to think there was a reason for this medical scare. My mother was so impressed with Lydia that she arranged for her to come out to the house and read for the family.

My mother set Lydia up in my bedroom, of all places. There were eighteen or twenty relatives and friends in the house, all waiting their turn to meet the psychic. One by one, they went in, emerging some time later with these glazed-over looks on their faces. Despite my mother's warnings to be on my best behavior, I smirked. I thought my entire family was nuts. I watched TV, trying to ignore the whole thing, although Lydia had startled me even before she started the readings. *If you're so good*, I thought to myself as she sat at the dining room table, drinking coffee and preparing to go upstairs, *tell me what I'm thinking now*. I was shocked when, a moment later, Lydia asked, "John, is there something you'd like to ask me?" "No," I stammered, "nothing, not a thing."

Lucky guess? At this point, I had to wonder. My cousin Roseann, known as "Little Ro," came out of her reading and told me, "John, she's good." Roseann was 30 but looked 15. Everyone who met her thought she was a teenager, and every psychic she went to talked about what boy she was going to meet and what college she was going to go to. Meanwhile, she was married and had a child. But this psychic was different. "She even knew I lost a baby," Roseann reported. She wanted me to go in and have a reading. I was old enough now. I resisted; I really had no interest. But Roseann kept it up and I finally relented, just to humor her, especially since she was paying. And I would prove Lydia wrong.

I sat down on the bed, and after a few pleasantries Lydia said to me, "You're the reason I'm here." I didn't know what to say. I'm fifteen years old and there's a woman in my bedroom telling me I'm the reason she's here. I thought maybe she just meant that it was my medical situation that had sparked her meeting my mother. But that's not what she meant. "I agreed to come here because I'm supposed to put you on this path in your life," she said. "What path?" I asked uncomfortably. She said, "You are very gifted. You have wonderful psychic abilities. You have highly evolved spiritual guides and they are ready to work with you. I was sent here today to introduce you to this world, to open you to your future." Lydia explained that she didn't normally come to people's houses but that something had led her here, and when she saw me in my mother's reading she knew I was the reason.

At this point I truly expected Rod Serling to walk out of my closet, accompanied by the theme music from *Twilight Zone*. I thought it was psychic shtick that she was laying on just a bit too thick. I'd always been such a skeptic, always pulling apart the things people like her were telling my mother. Now I was supposed to believe I was going to become one of them.

Lydia continued talking about my future in the spirit world, ignoring the fact that she was talking to a kid who aspired to an after-school job in the neighborhood deli and whose main concern was what girl he was going to go out with. But I decided I would have some fun with this. *I'll play with her,* I thought.

She began to read me. She started out with a few things that were generally specific to my age group, nothing that I even remember. Then she talked about some details about my family. They were on target, but she could have found this out from my mother. She asked if I had any questions. "No," I said, "I think I've heard enough." She said, "Really?" and laughed. "You don't want to know what's going to happen with Rebecca?"

That stopped me. I was somewhat precocious in those days, and was occasionally seeing a girl named Rebecca who was quite a few years older than I was. I kept it secret from my family because I'd have been in a serious jam if my mother knew. "I don't know who that is," I said with a straight face. She said, "Well, you don't have to acknowledge this, but I'm just going to give you the information." I said, "Go ahead, but it's not gonna make any sense to me." She said, "Well, you're not going to wind up with Rebecca. That's obvious. Nor is she going to wind up with Mark. He's the other person she's seeing, right?" I shrugged. I knew she was right.

"She's going to marry someone she works with. Who works with food. And I see him with her," she said. "She doesn't work with anybody who works with food," I replied smugly. Lydia just smiled knowingly.

A month or so later, Rebecca told me that she had broken up with Mark and was seeing someone new. I asked her where she'd met him. She told me she'd been working part-time as a waitress in a restaurant and had met him there. He was the chef.

Although I could only laugh at Lydia's preposterous prediction about my future life as a psychic, I couldn't deny that she had something here. And in retrospect, it's clear to me that she did what she set out to do. She put me on the path.

If I believed in coincidences—which I don't—I would say this is one: A few weeks after my encounter with Lydia, my great-aunt Louise visited and gave me one of those twenty-five-cent books they sell at the supermarket checkout counter, *How to Predict Your Future with Playing Cards*. I thought the timing of this little gift was pretty strange, but it seemed like harmless fun. I started doing "readings" for friends and relatives, predicting their futures after sorting through the playing cards. I would shuffle the cards, pick out seven of them, and then just make up a story. At least that's what I thought I was doing. I would say whatever came into my head. I'm not sure who was more amazed when many of the things I said turned out to be true. My cousins started calling and asking if they could come for another "reading," and would I mind if they brought ten friends with them? Of course, the idea that I had some unique ability never crossed my mind. I thought it was all in the cards.

I was curious, if not quite hooked. With Lydia's visit fresh in my mind, I went to the "occult" section of the library and began to read everything I could get my hands on, absorbing what I could about psychic phenomena, spiritualism, and metaphysics. I read about spirit guides, that we all have them, and that it was supposedly from them, not any playing cards, that I was getting my psychic information. As I read books by authors such as Ruth Montgomery, I began to wonder if it was possible that what Lydia said was true.

But I also thought, *Wait a minute, this isn't psychic stuff—this is normal*. These books were talking about the kinds of things I had been doing my whole life, using words like "clairvoyance" and "clairsentience" to describe abilities I thought everyone had. At school I began asking teachers I trusted whether they had ever been able to know things that hadn't happened yet, whether they ever felt as though they had been transported out of their bodies or thought they were flying during sleep. Of course, they would look at me and say,

"Uh, no." And I would start explaining some of the things that had happened to me since I was a little kid.

Susan Blind was one teacher who listened to me without passing judgment, and unknowingly had a hand in nudging me toward my life's work. I met her when my best friend, Mark Misiano, dragged me to an after-school meeting of the high school's Human Relations Club, for which she was faculty advisor. I sat inconspicuously in the back of the room, but at one point Ms. Blind looked at me as if she knew me and said, "John?" We had never met before, and she later said she had no idea how she knew my name. We became friends, and I considered her a role model: one of the few people I felt comfortable enough with to talk to in depth about what I was learning about myself. She didn't laugh or scoff at me. Her words were supportive—an example of the maxim that when the student is ready, the teacher appears.

Ms. Blind was a teacher and a friend, but she was not a *spiritual* teacher. The only person I have thought of in that way is someone I also met at this point. Her name is Sandi Anastasi, and she ran the Astrological Institute of Integrated Studies in Bay Shore, Long Island. (She has since moved to Port Charlotte, Florida, where she and her husband operate a New Age bookstore.) I began studying tarot and other metaphysical philosophies with Sandi, and she, too, told me that I was gifted. She gave a psychic development class, but told me not to come because, she said, I was too advanced.

Lydia Clar put me on this path but Sandi was the one who guided me. She helped me realize my strengths and weaknesses, and laid an important foundation: She helped me develop a sound understanding of metaphysics, and taught me the importance of keeping my ego in check.

Even as I explored this new universe, I was in most ways just a typical teenager and I didn't really take seriously the idea that I would one day make spirit communication my life's work. But I *was* curious about the legitimacy of psychics, especially on the subject of girlfriends. At one point I decided to go to another psychic, to kind of test what Lydia had said to me—not a test of her prediction about my supposed future in the field but of what she said about my life as a teenager with raging hormones. At least that's what I told myself.

My friend Mark's mother went to psychic seminars and gave my mother information on several practitioners. I decided to go to one, Maria D'Andrea, who used an old Nordic divination method known as rune stones to help her with readings. I went to see her and waited to see if she knew the same truth Lydia did regarding my social life. Without any prompting she began telling me just what Lydia had told me—about my future work. "You have a gift," she said. "You'll be doing this work." I thought, *Here we go again. Another one who wants me to join the ranks. Is this what they tell everyone?* She got up and called a woman who ran psychic seminars on Staten Island, New York. "You have to have this guy come work for you," she said into the phone. I thought, *What?* I had zero interest. Two weeks later I found myself at a psychic seminar on Staten Island, thinking, *What am I doing here? I can't do this for real. I do it for fun, I do it as a joke.* You know how one thing leads to another and things sometimes happen on their own, especially when you're young? Everyone told me I had nothing to lose by going to this woman with her psychic fairs. So I went.

Sheila Knies ran the show, which was located at a cultural center known as Snug Harbor. She took me into a cavernous room that had a dark, hollow, almost dungeonlike feel. "Okay," she said, "what is it that you do?" I said, "I don't know, really. I don't know what I do." She asked, "Why don't you show me?"

Oh, great, I thought. I don't even think I can do this and she wants to test me. I took out some tarot cards I'd brought with me (I'd graduated from regular old playing cards) and tried to "read" Sheila. I was terrible. But she smiled and asked me if I could stay. "Stay today?" I asked. "Yes, stay and read," she said. "Like do readings?" I said. "Yeah, I'd like to have you on," she said. "Are you serious?" I asked. "Yes, I'm very serious," she replied.

Years later, I asked Sheila why she had let me stay when I had given her a completely terrible reading. "You're right," she said. "The reading made no sense, no sense at all. But I know when people can do this and I could sense it from you. I knew you would be able to do it."

I did nine readings that day, and for the next year, I spent my Sundays at psychic fairs and seminars, telling people what was going to be happening in their futures. I sure didn't look the part. I was by far the youngest psychic in attendance and heard my share of "He's just a *kid*." No matter. I had no plans to take it further. My immediate plan was to graduate from high school, then go to college, get a job, have a family.

When I first started doing readings at the psychic fairs, it was always straight psychic work: what was going on in a person's life, what was coming up. I would use psychometry as my primary way to tune in, as I still do. I'd ask my client for a personal object I could hold onto to help key into his or her energy. Or I'd use cards or numerology, which are other ways of helping to unlock the door. As I got more comfortable with the process and the energies I was feeling—as I got better at my job, in essence—I began to feel that I was being led in another direction, to the point where I felt as though I was being physically interrupted by a new force. I'd be talking about what might be ahead for someone—a marriage, a baby, a job change, a move—when some other information would come in and just take over, something completely unrelated to what I was talking about, something very different from what I originally felt, as though I was tuning in two different radio stations simultaneously.

It started one day when I was working at a psychic fair and names suddenly began popping into my head. I'd always gotten validating information such as names, but this felt much different. "I'm getting the name Antonio," I said to my client, figuring it was a friend or relative of the woman I was reading. "I don't know if that name means anything to you." The woman said, "My grandfather was Antonio, but he's dead." Strange, I thought. Then, quickly, another name came to me. "Who's Maria?" The woman said, "Antonio's wife, my grandmother, but she's also dead." I asked, "Who's the 'L' sound that goes with them?" She said, "Maria's sister is Louise." I asked, "She's dead too?" She replied, "No, she's still alive."

I was as confused as the person sitting in front of me. "What does this mean?" she asked, staring in wonderment. *Good question,* I thought. I had to come up with something. "Well," I tried, "you know, these are people who were once important in your life or somehow connected with you in the past, and that's why I'm picking up on their names."

This happened more and more frequently, and I didn't like it. I found that it confused matters and somehow changed the rules of the game. (And a game was what I thought this was.) Despite my facile explanation, I knew deep down there was more to it. My early reading on psychic phenomena steered clear of mediumship, so I was groping in the dark. But one thing I knew on an instinctive, gut level was that I wasn't just tapping into this person's life but connecting with what felt like a very different energy. When this happened, I felt I was receiving information on two very distinct tracks, and I was trying (not very successfully) to join them together.

Mostly I tried to ignore it. It wasn't that connecting with the dead scared me; it was that it just didn't interest me very much. I was sixteen years old; why would I want to talk to dead people? Predicting the future: *that* was cool. The most impressive thing possible. In fact, I had so little curiosity about these names I found popping into my brain that I did not even entertain the possibility that I was reaching the dead. But I did need to rationalize it somehow, so I said, "These were people in your life. That's why I'm getting them." End of story. Now let's get back to that new job you're going to get.

The only thing was, it was more than just names and initials. It was vibrations. I knew these voices were different, and so was their source. And they kept getting louder and more insistent, more intrusive. I found it harder to ignore them. It was like a little kid coming up to you, wanting something while you're having a conversation. You say, "Not now," and five seconds later he comes back and says, "Now?" So there was this constant yanking feeling and I'd wind up trying to, in effect, have two conversations at once. The result was that I'd go off on tangents and the reading would get scattered. The whole thing left me confused and distracted. I'd read enough books by this point (and heard enough from Sandi Anastasi and Lydia Clar) to understand that whatever psychic skill I had was due to my ability to connect with my spirit guides. They were the ones giving me the information about people's lives. So who were these other guys? What the hell was going on here?

THE MAN WITH THE BARBER'S COMB

"Johnny, do that thing with the cards," my aunt Anna said to me teasingly one day. She wasn't taking me or "the work" seriously. And she wasn't alone; people in my life were having a hard time separating "little Johnny" from "John the psychic." But *I* was now starting to take it seriously, and I was determined to impress them. Anna sat down in front of me, and I concentrated. When I looked up I saw something that stunned me.

3

"What's the matter?" she asked. I said, "There's a woman standing behind you." Aunt Anna looked behind her. Nobody there. "Oh?" she said in a sing-songy voice, as if listening to a six-year-old tell a story. "And who is this woman?" I said, "I don't know." I described her before she disappeared. "She's in her sixties, kind of fleshy arms. She's smiling, very serene and peaceful. She's wearing a black dress and this kind of flower brooch. And she looks like she only has one leg. She reminds me of Uncle Sonny's Aunt Mary."

"Oh my God," my aunt said. "That sounds like my mother-in-law." I had never met this woman—she had died before I was born—but my aunt said she had lost a leg to diabetes. My aunt was amazed, and I was intrigued. Nothing like that had ever happened to me. I had no idea why this woman was there. Then, after she disappeared, my attention was drawn to the wall.

"Anna, now there's a man," I said. "A tall, slender man with salt-and-pepper hair, impeccably dressed in a beige-and-blue pinstripe suit and a pocket watch." I felt like he just materialized before me, as if he'd been beamed in through the wall. But the description meant nothing to my aunt. "I don't know who that is," she said. I looked at the man and began talking to him in my head. *She doesn't know who you are,* I said. *Tell me something, show me something.* At this, the man took out what looked like an old barber comb. Then he pointed to a clock surrounded by flowers. It said ten after two. Aunt Anna saw no man, no clock. She had no idea who he might be.

Afterward, she told everyone about what had happened. Her husband, Sonny, was there, and he took out his wallet and showed a picture of his mother. "That's who I saw!" I said. "That's her, that's the lady." Sonny's mother was wearing the same brooch I saw. She was even in the same pose, though she had both her legs in the picture. But no one seemed to know who the man was or what the significance of the clock might be.

Although I was excited, I wasn't shocked. This wasn't the first time I'd had an experience like this. When I was very young, five or six, I would see a little old man that I later learned was my grandfather, my mother's dad. He died in 1962, seven years before I was born. I would see him sitting at the table, next to my grandmother, and I dreamed of him often. One day when I was older, I was sitting on my bed doing homework, when I looked up and saw him standing in the doorway, smiling. "Don't worry, that's Grandpa," my grandmother would tell me casually. "He's just letting you know he's there, that he loves you and he's protecting you."

On December 29, 1987, one week after my encounters with the woman with the brooch and the man with the barber's comb pointing to a clock set at 2:10, a terrible thing happened. My uncle Carmine died of a heart attack. What made it especially hard, of course, was the vision of his death I'd had only three months before. It was in October of 1987, during one of my earliest experiences with mediation that I saw my Uncle Carmine walk in front of me and collapse, clutching his left arm. It looked like he was dying in front of my eyes. It was so strong, so vivid, and so disturbing. Was this meant as a warning? Was I supposed to intervene? I thought that maybe my mind was wandering, playing games, but then I realized the significance of having this vision during a meditation, when I knew the lines of communication with the spirit plane are clearest. I also knew that Uncle Carmine had a heart condition. I ran downstairs to tell my Aunt Roseann, whose sister was Carmine's wife. Roseann, whom we all called "Big Ro," wasn't sure what to do about it. We decided to call Carmine's daughter, "Little Ro." She told us that her father happened to be scheduled for a physical the next day. I considered the message delivered and waited to hear the outcome of the exam.

The next day, Carmine was given a clean bill of health. "They're missing something," I told Big Ro. She told me we had to leave it alone; the doctors knew what they were doing. I was convinced that I had predicted his death, and I was deeply disturbed that I could not prevent it.

I walked into the wake with my mother, my aunt, and a cousin, and we all stopped abruptly when we entered the room. There, at the foot of the coffin, was a clock surrounded by roses, exactly like the one I had seen the week before. The clock was set at 2:10, Carmine's time of death. It sounds morbid, but this was apparently some kind of funeral tradition. The four of us were speechless.

At the wake, I was sitting by myself when I was struck by an overpowering piece of information: *That man was his father*. The natty-looking man with the barber comb was Carmine's father. I had to tell Aunt Anna. As I stood up, she was headed down the aisle, looking for *me*. "Johnny, I'll bet you that man was his father," she told me with more excitement than you usually see at a wake. "Oh my God, I was just coming to tell *you* that," I said. "What made you think that?" Anna said she didn't know; the thought just came over her, as if she just *knew* this. Carmine was her brother-in-law, and she'd never known his father.

I needed confirmation. I had to know if the man with the barber comb was Carmine's father. I needed to find someone who could describe him. I couldn't ask Theresa, his widow. Not the right time or place. I asked one of my cousins. She didn't know anything. Anna and I went to another cousin. "Phyllis, can you describe your dad's dad for me? What did he look like?"

Phyllis described an old man who could have been anybody. Anyway, the man I'd seen was younger. "He was a good dresser, I remember," she said. "Uh-huh," I said. Too inconclusive for me. "What did he do?" Anna asked. "He was a barber," Phyllis said. Anna looked at me. "The comb," she said.

I've always felt that my Uncle Carmine started it—really started it. It's as if when he passed, he was saying, "Johnny's not plugged in enough," and sort of went over to my "Other Side" switch and plugged me in, because after that it was like the lights came on and the Other Side really started coming through with messages in the form of sounds and images and feelings that came into my head as if they were placed there by an unseen force.

Not that I was ready for it. Nor did enlightenment come without a price. There was a lesson to be learned, and it was a painful one. As a child I was always a little bit afraid of Carmine. I shied away from him. My mother thought it was because he was a very loud, demonstrative person, but that wasn't it. Carmine was extremely generous, and especially good to me. He was always bringing me things. As a kid (I admit this) I collected *Charlie's Angels* cards. And he once brought me an entire box of those cards. He's the one who gave me the *"I Dream of Jeannie"* bottle. That's the kind of guy he was. Yet I was always vaguely uncomfortable around him, and I have come to think that it's because I somehow knew I was going to be connected to his passing, that I was going to see it and go through it in this strangely intimate and traumatic way.

In the weeks and months after he died, I struggled with the mixed message of Carmine's passing. I had decided by now that my special ability—whatever level of aptitude it ultimately reached—was meant to be something more than a parlor game. I was supposed to use it to help people. But I couldn't understand why, if this was so, I had been unable to help my uncle. I had decided to invest myself emotionally in this, to open my heart and soul to it. And here I had failed the first time out—or *it* had failed. Failed miserably, tragically. There was no doubt in my mind that I had been informed of his death ahead of time: first, the vision of him having a heart attack, then his father coming to me, pointing to the clock only a week before he died. But what was the point of being shown something so horrible if I couldn't use this information to prevent it from happening? It was like knowing someone was going to fall off a cliff, getting up to the cliff, getting to the person, then watching him slip out of your hands. You're left with the feeling that you are somehow responsible. And that feeling haunted me for quite some time.

I talked about this with my mother. "I don't understand why I was shown this," I said one day in her bedroom. She was setting her hair, and I was looking at her reflection in the mirror.

"Johnny," she said, "you have to know there is a higher power here. You're just given an ability to help, but you're not in control. No matter how good you are, or how good you become, you're only a small part of the big picture: a facilitator, a messenger, a helper."

"I never really thought much about death before, but it really stinks," I said. "You know, I think people should be given one last time. There should be a way to give people one last time to talk to the people in their lives. One chance to say their good-byes after they've gone to the Other Side."

"Well, that's what makes death death," my mother said. "The finality of it."

"Here's my idea: Five days and five hours after death, you get a one-hour window. You get to reconnect with your family and friends.

You can tell them good-bye, tell them you love them, tell them anything you want."

I saw my mother's face in the mirror, and she was just smiling. "You're such an optimist," she said. "I hope you never lose that."

"One last time," I said, liking the sound of it.

So maybe death was not the end. Maybe these names coming through to me were the spirits of souls gone to the Other Side. I began to play with that idea in my head, and after Uncle Carmine passed, it really kicked in. Names and initials would come through louder and more insistently than before, and they came with what I can only describe as a feeling—a feeling of contentment, love, and peace.

I wanted to learn as much as I could about after-death communication. Besides reading, I looked for ways to study the spirit world firsthand. I had started out considering the possibility that I was mind reading, a phenomenal feat in itself, if not quite on the level of communicating with the dead. But the more I read, and the more validating information I got from what I considered the Other Side, the more convinced I became.

I continued my studies of tarot, numerology, and meditation with Sandi Anastasi, while looking for ways to better understand the Other Side and how to reach it. On her wall, Sandi had a list of psychics and mediums. My eye caught a listing for a medium who lived not far from my home. Her name was Shelley Peck. I decided to call her for an appointment; I realized that while I was connecting people with the spirit world, I had only been read myself by psychics, never once by a medium. We spoke for several hours on the phone, but when I showed up (driven by my uncle Joey) Shelley was startled by my age; I was only sixteen. "I can't read you," she said "You're too young." Well, she did anyway, and we became fast friends and colleagues.

One day I called Shelley and asked her if she would lead me through a meditation to introduce me to my spirit guides. I was at the point now where I wanted to know who they were. I needed a more direct connection with them. I needed to meet them.

We started with a "guided visualization," which is something like hypnosis. Shelley guided me through a series of exercises involving mental imagery to help me unlock the doors of my unconscious mind so that I could connect with my guides—literally meet them.

Through these visualization techniques, I felt myself transported to a different plane of consciousness. I found that I had five guides plus a master guide. A master guide is a spirit who is assigned to you from the day you're born until the day you pass to the Other Side. When I visualized my guides, one seemed to be a kind of Oriental monk. Another was a sort of goofy teenager. Then, when I visualized my master guide, I saw all kinds of Indian symbolism: I saw an Indian with a huge headdress on. And I thought, *What a bunch of crap.* Not only did it seem like the worst cliché, but there was no way I would have an Indian as a spirit guide, let alone my master guide. I never shared my mother's love of Indian lore and symbols. She had statues around the house, and I never liked them.

In this trancelike state, I told Shelley what I was seeing. "This guy is telling me that he's going to make his presence known to me," I said. "He says he knows I need proof, and that I'll find the proof in my family." Despite my skepticism, Shelley was confident this would prove out. And I was thinking, *Oh great, this Indian dude's gonna pop out at me during study hall at school.*

At home one afternoon about two weeks later, I felt a powerful impulse to go to the garage. So I went to the garage. *All right,* I thought, *I'm in the garage. Why am I in the garage?* Now something told me, "Go to the shelf." I went to the shelf. I was drawn to a big box, and when I opened it I saw that it was filled with photo albums. I went right to one album in particular, one filled with pictures of my parents from the early years of their marriage, each with a caption underneath and a date. I began flipping through it and stopped at a page that had a picture that seemed out of place. Between a picture of my mother, pregnant with me, and one of my father, was a very faded photograph of what seemed to be a downcast face, almost a sad-clown face without the makeup and rubber nose. *What the hell is this?* I thought. What made it even stranger was that the caption under it said, "Prin and Jack, 1968." (My mother's nickname was Prin, short for Princess. Her real name was Perinda.)

I showed the album to my mother, minus the photo, and asked her what picture she remembered being in that spot. She said the photos on the page were snapped during a vacation she and my father had taken shortly before I was born, and the caption went with a picture of the two of them. "Where's that picture?" she asked. I showed her the faded image of the clown. "This is it," I said. "No it's not," she said. "I don't know what that is, but the picture that's supposed to be here is a picture of me and your father together in front of the car. Look. See?" She pointed to the caption.

I left the photo in my room. When I looked at it a few days later, I saw that it had changed. The face was now clearly that of an Indian, headdress and all. You could have knocked me over with a feather. To this day, I am amazed when I look at that picture. I would be lying if I said I understood how we are matched with our spirit guides. I certainly would not have chosen an Indian chief to be my master guide. But it has been my assumption since that day that this was indeed my master guide showing himself to me. His purpose was to give me the confirmation he knew I needed. He wanted to bolster my fledgling interest in the spirit world and encourage me to continue on this path.

It worked. I was becoming consumed by a need to know more. All this information—the books I read, the conversations I had with more experienced psychics and mediums, the personal experiences that came with them—was like an ocean of knowledge and I was totally immersed in it. Every day brought something new.

It was around this time that I started having what could be called premonitions about negative news events. Often this took the form of an abrupt but fleeting depression occurring about three to five days before a major world disaster. I would get moody, short with people, even teary. People couldn't talk to me. Then, a few days later, I would hear some terrible news. The first time this happened was in January 1986 when the space shuttle Challenger exploded. It would later happen with several tragedies: the Pan Am 103 disaster in Scotland, and the terrorist bombings in Oklahoma City and at the World Trade Center.

I assumed this information was coming, unsolicited, from my spirit guides. So when I went to a psychic fair, where I would have to actively try to draw information from them, I used a technique to bring them closer. I visualized my guides as helium balloons up in the sky. And I would imagine pulling them in close to me, so that when I was doing a reading I would feel them all around me.

At the same time, I was grappling with the messages from that other track: the Other Side. I was now past the point when I could ignore them. In fact, they were beginning to take over. I would sit down for a psychic reading—I billed myself strictly as a psychic, not a medium—and have to begin by apologizing to people. I know you're here for a psychic reading, I would say. I know you want to hear about the events going on in your life and what might be coming up for you. But I'm really sorry, I have this ability to connect with people on the Other Side and they might interrupt us. So let's just get that out of the way first.

Some people looked at me as if I were from another planet. Others waited to hear what might come next. More often than not, spirits would come through with information, and most of my clients would be shocked. This was not what they expected, not what they signed up for, and they had no idea what to make of it. But there were some who, if I happened to hit on something very specific, would begin to cry, and hug me and thank me. I was just as unprepared for this as they were to have some teenage kid tell them their departed loved ones had dropped by to send their regards.

The messages I received at this point early in my development were often very cryptic and disjointed. The language is very symbolic, rarely literal, and it would take years for me to understand it with any reliability or fluency. It started out simple, as with any second language. But unlike a Berlitz course, I was teaching myself, without the benefit of either an instructor or a textbook. I had to find my own way and make my own interpretations. Flowers were the first symbols I got, but I had to figure out what they meant. I would be shown a white flower, and found that this seemed to happen when my client was celebrating an event such as a birthday. Eventually I deduced that the white flower was a sign of congratulations.

But it was a struggle, and I was not always in the right frame of mind to pick up the signs. One Sunday, I was working at a psychic fair at a Holiday Inn and had before me a woman who was dressed completely in black: black dress, black hat, black stockings, black shoes, even black-rimmed glasses. She was from California, I found out later, and staying with her mother. She had been driving by the Holiday Inn, decided to stop in for a cup of tea, then saw the sign, "Psychic Fair," and went downstairs. She later told me she saw my name and was drawn to me.

Early in the reading, I said a name and she started crying hysterically. I asked what was wrong, and she said, "That's my father." I figured she'd just had a fight with her father, but then she told me her father had just died. She was in New York for the funeral. I realized that the information wasn't *about* her father. It was coming *from* him. She had not had a chance to say goodbye, and he was coming through saying it was all right, she shouldn't feel bad. (This is a great example of how legitimate psychics or mediums don't study their clients' appearance for clues, but rather save all their energy for tuning in to that which can't be seen. This woman was clearly dressed for a funeral, but I was oblivious.)

Generally, I resisted the Other Side at psychic fairs because the readings were only fifteen minutes long, and I wasn't that quick then. Usually the information was like drip, drip, drip. But in this case, I began hitting on details. I picked up on her grandmother, and then her grandfather came through, and her father. The woman hugged me when she left and came back the next day with her mother, her sister, and her aunt, delaying her flight back to California to have another reading. That experience helped me open up more and was a turning point in my becoming not just a psychic but a medium. When she hugged me, I realized for the first time how important this work could be.

I t wasn't until I was nineteen—four years after I'd first met Lydia Clar—that the importance of all this truly hit me where I lived. I'd become convinced there were spirit guides and that there was life after death. The validation for me was in all the people I'd read, mostly at psychic fairs. But it didn't have a deep meaning for me until my mother passed.

She had been complaining about an increasingly bad pain around her shoulders for some time when she was diagnosed with lung cancer in April of 1989. She had surgery, she had chemotherapy, she had radiation, but it was pretty clear her chances were poor. She was a heavy smoker and her cancer was too advanced. Right from the start, we were told that she had six months to live by a doctor who also told those of us who were closest to her that we had to pretend that everything was going to be fine. The doctor told my mother that she had a chance. And under the doctor's instructions,

5

I told her she would be all right. You're going to beat this, I said. But she knew the truth: I had inadvertently let it slip out on the way to the doctor's office that day—even before we got the diagnosis.

"Who's Abe?" I had said in the car. Someone was coming through to me and his name was Abe. My cousin Lil' Ro was in the back seat, and she said, "That was my father's nickname, down at his job. They called him Abe." Her father was my uncle Carmine. And he was telling me to tell my mother not to believe whatever the doctor was going to tell her. "Ma," I said, "I'm picking up this really big force. The doctors are going to tell you something and this Abe is telling me to tell you don't believe them. They're lying to you." That night, after getting the bad news, it wasn't the cancer diagnosis she took as a lie but the doctor's assurance that she could beat it. She told me she knew she was terminal. And she told me how sad she was that she wouldn't live to see my twenty-first birthday. A few weeks later she gave me a gold ring and a matching diamond bracelet for a birthday that was nearly a year away.

Several months later, with my mother's condition deteriorating rapidly, we had a conversation about reaching each other once she passed to the Other Side. "When I get there, I won't be gone," she told me. "I'll talk to you all the time."

"Ma, it's not going to be like that," I told her. "It won't be that easy coming through to me because I won't be able to be objective. I'll be constantly wondering if I'm wanting it so badly that I'm only imagining it."

"I can't believe you're not going to even talk to me," she said.

"It's not that. It's that it would be easier for me to believe if it comes through another medium." Still, though I felt this was the best thing to do in the long run, I wanted her to come through to me directly with a sign soon after she passed, just to let me know she had arrived on the Other Side and was all right.

My mother died at four in the morning on October 5. We were all surrounding her bed at home—me, her mother and sisters, my cousins—and the emotion was heavy. As soon as she passed, I walked out of her bedroom and into mine, sat down on the bed and looked

out the window. It was a crystal-clear night. I began to talk to my
mother, acting as a kind of psychic coach to ease her transition to
the Other Side. "Right about now," I said to her, "your father and
probably Uncle Carmine will be there to greet you on the Other Side.
You should go toward the light. And you shouldn't worry about the
emotions that you're sensing in your room. Don't be afraid. You're
going to be okay." And then, I asked her to give me a sign that she
was all right. "It's got to be something very specific," I told her.
"Nothing I can shoot down and say I'm just imagining it." I decided
on a white bird. "But it's got to be very personal to me," I emphasized
again. "Like on *my* car or on *my* windowsill."

But even as I told her all this, a part of me wondered if what I
was saying was true. Would she be okay? Would I? I needed to know
that all this "Other Side" business was real. I put it all on the white
bird. If she sent it to me, I would know.

Later that day, Shelley Peck called to extend her sympathy. But
there was more. She said she had "a bunch of messages for me." I
thought she meant messages of condolence from people we knew
from the psychic fairs. No, she said. Messages from my mother. "All
right," I said, sitting down on my bed. I put my feet up and rested
my head against the headboard. "Go ahead." But as soon as I said
that, I had second thoughts. "Hold on," I told Shelley. "I don't think
I'm ready to hear this yet."

"No, no, you have to hear this," Shelley insisted. "She's showing
me something symbolic of Jesus Christ. A wooden statue. She's telling
me it was hand-carved in Italy."

"I don't know what that is," I said, sounding like one of our
clients.

"It's Jesus Christ and the Blessed Mother and something else."

"I still don't know what you're talking about."

"She's saying there's something else religious. Something from her
room that's now in your room."

I looked around my room. "I don't see anything."

"Keep looking."

"I *am* looking, Shelley," I said, getting frustrated and a bit annoyed. "There's nothing here like you're describing."

"There is," she insisted.

"There's not." I began to argue with her. "You're wrong. I'm looking everywhere. There's nothing."

"She's telling me very clearly there is. It's there."

"There's nothing religious that was in my mother's room . . . Oh my God. It's right here."

"I told you," Shelley said. "What is it?"

It was a picture of the Blessed Mother and the Sacred Heart, and the reason I hadn't seen it was because it was behind my head, taped to my headboard. The headboard was actually a mirror that had been atop the bureau opposite my mother's bed in her room. I had taken it out of her room a few weeks before because I didn't want her to see herself deteriorating. The picture had come with it.

Shelley had more. "She's telling me that you brought her something back from Venezuela when you went there. This is weird. I'm getting a statue, but it's not like the normal statue you would buy of the Blessed Mother."

"Yes," I said. "I went to Venezuela and I bought her a handblown statue of the Blessed Mother." But I still didn't know what the hand-carved statue from Italy was about. And more than that, I was preoccupied with the white bird. Why would my mother give Shelley all this other information and not give me the sign I wanted?

My cousin was to be married two days later. My mother had told everyone that no matter what happened to her, she wanted the wedding to go on as planned. We actually put off her funeral two days to accommodate her wishes. I spent the whole wedding desperately looking for a white bird, keeping it to myself to make sure nobody arranged anything just to make me feel better. My mother was such a strong energy that I had no doubt she would do what we'd agreed. But the wedding ended without any white birds appearing, and I went back to helping make the final arrangements for my mother's wake. When Lil' Ro asked me what kind of flowers I wanted, I asked her to take care of it for me. "Whatever's appropriate," I said.

It was at the wake that I discovered the wooden statue Shelley had told me about during our phone conversation. It was an over-sized, hand-carved rosary from Italy that my mother's sister Rachel bought to hang on the inside of the casket. Shelley's abilities floored me, but I still wanted those white birds.

On the third and last day of the wake, as the casket was being moved from the funeral home to the church, one of my cousins, who was especially close to my mother, came over and put his arm around my shoulder. "John, I'm here for you," he said as we stood alone in the back of the room. He remarked on all the flowers that had been sent to the wake. "I can't believe how many there are," he said. "Yours stand out the most." I said, "Roseann and Joey picked them out." He said, "It's not just the flowers. It's those beautiful white birds." I looked at him and said, "What?"

"Those beautiful white birds on your flowers," he repeated.

I went over to the flowers and saw that he was right—there were two white birds that I had completely overlooked for three days. I had even moved one of them to get at a certain rose I wanted to give my grandmother. Suddenly I realized the significance of my cousin's exact words. He said, "White birds on *your* flowers." That was my mother's way of making them personal to me—how would my cousin know they were "my" flowers? And how could I have missed them? All I can say is sometimes we miss the obvious. I went over to the birds, picked one out and gave it to my cousin.

The next day, curious, I called the florist and asked why there had been white birds on those particular flowers. Were they the usual adornments for an arrangement for a wake? Had they been re-quested? The florist seemed surprised and embarrassed, saying that he normally put those white birds on orders for celebratory events, not for wakes. He explained that he was serving a number of confir-mation parties the day these flowers were ordered and one of the people in the shop must have mistakenly put the birds on this ar-rangement. He apologized profusely, assuming I was calling to com-plain. "No, no," I explained. "The flowers were fine. And the birds were beautiful."

The birds made my mother's death real to me. It was the moment I started to grieve. Until then, I had been operating in a fog, making arrangements, doing what I had to do, keeping myself together—looking so unlike the anguished only child that someone actually came up to me at the wake and asked, "Which one's her son?" But seeing those white birds, holding them in my hand, made me think, *Oh, my God, she did this from the Other Side, which means she's really dead. She's not here.* In order to accept that sign, I had to accept that she was gone.

Before my mother died, she made me promise two things: one, that her mother would be treated "like a queen," and two, that the parties would continue. We had always had a lot of family parties, big, catered gatherings in backyards and living rooms with everyone invited, friends, relatives, neighbors. With my mother's dying wish in mind, I began planning a party for my grandmother's birthday in January, even though it was only a month since my mother passed, and the party would take place just three months afterward. But before I got too far I began considering canceling the party. Despite my mother's wishes, I was feeling disrespectful and guilty. I asked my mother if I was doing the right thing.

A few days later, she came to me in a dream. Dreams are spirits' way of communicating with us directly. It is important to say that not every dream of a dead relative is a visit; many are our way of dealing with the loss. But there is a fairly simple way to distinguish between a dream that is a visit from someone on the Other Side and a dream that is just a dream. A *visit* is profound, a gift. It feels incredibly vivid and real, and stays with us much longer than a standard dream. While the details of most dreams dissolve from memory within a few hours, a visit will be remembered clearly years later. But it doesn't mean that everything in a dream-visit will make perfect sense.

In her visit, my mother came to me in a bar. I don't drink. I begin the dream in the downtown area of the town I grew up in, sweeping the sidewalk outside the bar on a crisp autumn day. Several people walk by me as I sweep, all of whom I recognize as people who have passed, including two young people I went to school with.

I go inside the bar, sit on a stool, and order a Pepsi. At the opposite end of the bar are my grandmother and my mother's youngest sister, both still alive. There are others in the bar but I don't recognize them. The door opens and a gust of wind brings in a swirl of just-fallen leaves. They are followed by my mother. She walks through the door looking radiant, glowing, her sickness and at least ten years stripped away. She comes wrapped in a striking purple coat that I recognize.

I don't say anything right away but think, *What are you doing here? You're dead.* She smiles at me and says, "I had to come and tell you I love you and it's beautiful where I am. And that I'm okay."

"But Ma, you're dead," I say again. She looks at me, as if to say, "You should know better—you of all people." Again, I ask her why she's here. She tells me she needed to tell me she is still with me and that she's proud of what I'm doing. I ask her what she means and she says, "The party. I'm so excited. I can't wait to come."

I ask my mother what my future has in store for me. She shakes her head from side to side. She lets me know that she can't tell me, but that she will be with me always and that she will let me know that from time to time.

At this point in the dream, I question what is really happening here. Even though I'd already had many encounters with spirits—including several personal paranormal experiences, such as the episodes with Uncle Carmine—I am skeptical that this is anything but a dream. (Whether in dreams or through spirit messages, to this day I have different standards for myself. I am not nearly as skeptical about other people as I am about myself because I am always wondering if I am somehow tricking myself.)

"Am I making this up?" I ask. "Is this my own subconscious giving me permission to have this party?" My mother looks at me and says, "This party's going to be great."

Now she walks toward my grandmother. And my grandmother starts to disappear. My aunt grabs on to my grandmother and screams, "No! You can't have her!" The next thing is wordless. It is my mother saying *I'll leave her now but I'm going to have to come back for her.* My grandmother begins to reappear.

At this point, I say to my mother, "I know you're here. But what is this really?"

My mother smiles. "Johnny," she says, "this is *your* one last time."

She lets this sink in for a moment. It's been two years since we had that conversation when I said that everyone should get "one last time" to connect with their loved ones after they've gone to the Other Side. And she had just smiled and told me how cute I was.

As I'm taking all this in, she starts for the exit. When she gets to the door, she turns around, runs her fingers up and down the collar of her purple coat and says, coyly, "Would you pick up this coat?" Ending this profound interlude on that cryptic remark, she smiles and walks out the door.

As my mother left, I bolted up in bed. It was morning. I realized I had been crying. My pillow was soaked. I was soaked. I ran downstairs and told my grandmother and my aunt what had just happened. (Everything except the part about my mother coming for my grandmother.) We were all stunned, but still I wondered: was that a visit, or just an episode my psyche dreamed up—literally—to make me feel better?

Half an hour later, I had a sudden urge to go to the deli in town for an egg sandwich, the kind you just can't make as well at home. The deli was in a strip mall that included the video store where I worked and a dry cleaner. As I pulled into the parking lot, I saw the woman who ran the dry cleaner wave to me, and I waved back. Then she motioned for me to come inside. I thought she needed change— we were always going back and forth when we needed change—but when I went inside, she came out of the back carrying a garment in a plastic bag. It was my mother's purple coat. I was speechless. (I still am when I think about it.) "Where's your mom been?" the dry cleaner asked. "She brought this in back in April"—April was when my mother was diagnosed with cancer—"and never came for it. She paid for it."

I remembered that my aunt had noticed the purple coat was missing when we were going through my mother's clothes after she passed. We assumed my mother had given it away, and my aunt joked that she wished it was still in the closet: she could have used a nice winter coat like that. But it seems my mother had more important plans for the coat. I thought it was very interesting that she had paid for the dry-cleaning in advance.

The purple coat was, and remains, the most profound personal validation I have received. Without it, to this day I would question whether my mother had actually come through with my "one last time," assuring me all was well on the Other Side and that we should go on with our lives, starting with the party for my grandmother. The way she playfully fingered the coat and then arranged for me to "pick it up" was her way of saying, "This is real. And I'm going to prove it to you."

In retrospect, I now see how my mother's passing showed me how important after-death communications are to those left behind. If I needed it, I assumed most people do. This was more than fun and games, entertainment at psychic "fairs." And in that way, my mother showed me the path I needed to be on. But while her visit did mark a turning point for me, I also have to say that I didn't fully realize it right away. That didn't come until I got past the anger that overwhelmed me during those months. Though the purple coat dream was an exhilarating moment, it did not diminish the rage I felt that God had taken my best friend, and that with all my supposed abilities I could do nothing to stop it, just as I had not been able to intervene in my uncle Carmine's passing.

My mother's doctor had told me that if her cancer had been detected earlier, she would have had a better chance. That's not something you tell a psychic. It was especially disturbing because she had gone months with pains that were misdiagnosed. Why hadn't I seen it? Why did God give me this ability if I couldn't use it to help those closest to me? Was this some kind of cosmic joke?

I was so confused and hurt that I stopped my psychic work altogether. When a regular customer came into the video store and asked for my help—her brother-in-law was missing—I coldly said, "No. I don't do that work anymore," and walked away. But as I was driving home a few hours later, I replayed that abrupt conversation over in my head and immediately heard my mother say, "Johnny, God granted you a beautiful gift. Use it wisely. You won't be able to make everyone happy, but if you can help just one person in your lifetime, then it is all worth it." Damn, I thought. I didn't want to hear it. I turned the music up in the car to stop these thoughts.

When I got home, I saw my next-door neighbor, Lisa, beckon me over. Before I could even get out of the car, she tossed an orange jacket in my hands and asked, "What do you get?" I was in no mood for psychic parlor games about the next guy in her life. As I went to put the jacket down I heard the word "missing." It was as if someone had pressed the "play" button on a tape recorder. I got a man's name, the fact that he drowned, that he was married and was out with another woman, that she also drowned, and when they would be found. It turned out that this man was the same missing person the woman in the video store had asked for my help in finding. He was an old friend of Lisa's parents. All the messages I received turned out to be accurate, and when I met the man's wife, she thanked me. Though the circumstances were of course painful for her, she said it helped bring her closure. She told me, "You have a remarkable gift. Use it wisely and know that even if you can help one person, it's worth it." Was this echo my mom's way of letting me know she had orchestrated the whole thing—and that the message was worth repeating? What I do know is that this experience helped me get past my anger and guide me back on track.

PART II

ENCOUNTERS WITH
THE OTHER SIDE

I want you to know how I do what I do. Of course, it's very difficult to explain in any kind of scientific way, so maybe a better way to put it is to say that I want you to know *what* I do—beyond simply saying I talk to the dead. Like other psychics and mediums, I hear sounds, see images, and—the most difficult to explain—feel thoughts and sensations that are put into my mind and body by spirits on the Other Side. They do this in order to convey messages to people they have left behind on the physical plane.

In some cases, I can give a good reading simply by passing on what I'm hearing, seeing, and feeling. But in most instances, I must interpret the information so that the meaning is understood. I call the entire process "psychic sign language." What I've been able to do in the years since I started this work is to become more fluent in understanding the symbols, making it easier for me to validate the presence of spirits.

And ultimately, that is one of their chief goals: to convey enough specific, irrefutable information to prove that this is real and that they are actually still here with us, albeit not physically. Once they've done that, they've gone a long way toward achieving their greater purpose: making those of us on this side understand that they did not disappear into some black hole of nonexistence when they "died," but that they have only passed into another form—as we all will someday. They communicate with us not only to let us know they are fine—as we will also be when we get there—but to assure us that they are still involved in our lives, whether it's by acknowledging a birth of a baby or by remarking that they like a new hairstyle.

All of us—we in physical bodies and those in the spirit world—are made up of energy expressed as atoms and molecules spinning and vibrating at certain speeds. The energy of spirits vibrates at a very high rate, while ours goes much slower because we are in physical bodies. How we bridge the gap dictates how well communications traverse these two dimensions. That's the job of a medium.

For spirits to come through, they must slow their vibrational rate of energy. Think of the blades on a helicopter. You can't see that there are four of them because they are spinning too fast. That's how I view the energy of the spirits. What happens during a reading is that as the spirits slow down their energies, I speed mine up. Communication is what happens in that space in between. But because there is that space, that gap, communication is never easy and rarely clear. There is also the fact that spirits no longer have physical bodies to facilitate communication. They have no tongues or vocal cords to pronounce words. Instead, through their energies, they place thoughts and sights and sounds in my mind. I am their mouthpiece. Though I expected to hear a great voice from beyond when I first started this work, I soon realized that it is my own voice I hear—but their thoughts and feelings.

Because both sides must expend so much energy to make this happen, the communication is very difficult and can't be sustained for more than a few minutes. To switch metaphors, it's as if you have to go to the bottom of a twelve-foot-deep swimming pool to meet your loved one. You can do it, but it takes a lot of energy to get there and after a few seconds, you have to float back to the top for air.

So how does it happen? While it's true that I naturally attract the energies of spirits—they know I can perceive, understand, and convey their meaning—I make sure I do everything possible to maximize that ability. To do this, I go through a series of exercises to raise my vibrations to meet those of the spirits.

First, I meditate. I center myself so that my energies are as focused as they can be. As a Catholic, I also pray the rosary; I pray that I will be able to deliver messages clearly and that people will be receptive to those messages. I started doing this after many spirits showed me rosary beads turning into musical notes, a symbolic message that the rosary (and any intense and repetitive prayer, whatever one's faith) is almost literally music to their ears. It brings us closer to them, and them closer to us. Everyone has the ability to receive these energies to some degree. What I have is the ability to look at them with a different set of eyes, feel them with a different set of hands, and listen to them with a different set of ears than most people.

It is not a conversational language, though many believe it is. When I do a reading, people might think I'm repeating exactly what I'm hearing. But what I am actually doing is delivering and interpreting symbolic information as fast as I can keep up with it. If it were truly conversational, I would be a lot more accurate than I am. It's just not that simple. Rather than just talking and listening, the tools of my trade are my psychic senses. Just as we use the five basic human senses—sight, sound, touch, smell, and taste—a medium uses the same basic senses, only psychically.

Here is a description of each of these senses:

Clairaudience (clear hearing)—I am able to hear sounds, including voices, that come from the spirits. Mostly, I hear my own voice—my mind's voice—rather than the voice of the person whose spirit is coming through, though I have on occasion heard messages from a male, female, or even my mother's voice. Imagine that while you are reading this you are also thinking about whether or not you left the oven on. That's your mind's voice. That's how spirit messages sound to me.

Clairvoyance (clear seeing)—This allows spirits to show me objects, symbols, and scenes. Sometimes these are meant literally, as in the image of a car to convey to me that the spirit passed in a car accident. Other times the image is more symbolic. That same car might be shown to me as a symbol of something else. For example, a spirit might show me a Ford to get me to say that name. And to use the example above about thinking about whether you turned the oven off, your mind might show you the oven. That's how I see these images. Clairvoyance is also how spirits show me what they looked like while in the physical body, either by showing me themselves or someone I can identify who fits the same description.

Clairsentience (clear sensing)—This is feeling or sensing a spirit's message. This can take a variety of forms. It's how spirits convey emotions they felt or are feeling, as well as physical feelings to show me what they were feeling prior to death and after. This sometimes includes "sympathetic pain," where I "feel" what parts of their physical bodies were the focus of whatever problems they had. Through clairsentience I have felt chest pains, stomach pains, joint pains. In other cases I have felt emotions ranging from love to sorrow.

Clairalience (clear smelling) and clairhambience (clear tasting)—I get smells and tastes that help me convey validating messages. Clairalience is sometimes referred to by mediums as "smelling them," whether it be a perfume, a cigar, or some other scent closely associated with the person now in spirit.

A good reading depends on my using all these senses at once, putting together the various symbols, sounds, and feelings and interpreting them into a coherent message. This is why my work can be extremely draining. It may seem as if I'm just sitting there pulling things out of the air and relating them, but my brain is working hard, trying to catch what can be a bombardment of thoughts and images and interpret them.

Some things, of course, are easily interpreted. Names, for instance. As long as I am hearing it correctly, there's no doubt what it means. It's either the name of the spirit, or that of someone the spirit is acknowledging. The trick is distinguishing between the two. Sometimes the spirit will help by giving me, for instance, a feeling of going up to indicate someone in the generations above: parents, grandparents, aunts, uncles. Or a parallel feeling, to the side of the client, if I am meant to convey a brother or sister, a cousin, or a friend. To indicate a child, the spirit will focus my energies downward. It's one example of clairsentience.

Oftentimes, I get a combination of feelings that I use to decipher the identity of either the spirit or the person the spirit is referring to. A lighter, softer feeling tends to indicate a female, while a stronger, dominant presence indicates a male. (There are, of course, exceptions in the cases of men who come through more gently and women who are strong and dominant.)

In each case, I will tell the client what I am feeling to make it easier for him or her to identify the spirit. Sometimes I use the client as a guide. "Tom was my brother," he might say, giving the reading an early context by indicating that Tom is the one coming through. But other times, the *spirit* will be the guide. For example, if my client says, "Tom was my brother," I might say, "Okay, but this is a different Tom, because he's definitely showing me he's above you on the family tree."

Besides those of people, I have heard all kinds of names—of places, songs, movies. I also hear phrases. But the clarity varies wildly. Very few things come in loud and clear, as if they've been handed to me in lightning bolts on a tablet and I can just read it: *This just in from the Other Side.* Clairaudience means "clear hearing," but in reality it is far from that.

With names, for instance, sometimes I get the whole thing, other times just an initial or a sound. Sometimes it's analogous to a radio with very heavy static. You hear a voice, but it's not clear and you try to catch a word here or there. Other times the messages are very faint, like a whisper, or come and go incredibly fast. You catch it for a split second as it rushes by, like a train. And still other times it's like a voice that keeps breaking up. If a spirit were to try to give me the name James, I might just get the "J" sound or a "J-S" sound. "Ellen" might come through with the "L" sound strongest, or

"L-N." By experience, I would probably know that the spirit is not giving an "L" initial, indicating it's a name that begins with that letter, but that it's the dominant sound. So I would give that as Ellen or Ellie or some variation. "Oscar" would come through as an "S," the dominant sound. With experience, I have become sharper at picking the names out, better at differentiating between, say, "Ellen" and "Helen," or between "Jack" and "Jacques." I might be off on the full name, but I virtually always get the initial or the sound. Over the years I've been able to turn up the volume, but that hasn't made it any easier to understand the messages. If there was one thing I would ask the spirits, it would be to slow down and speak more clearly.

Images are next on the scale of difficulty, but for a different reason. It's not that I don't see them well, but that they are often meant symbolically and it's up to me (with the help of my client, who knows what the big picture looks like) to figure out what they mean. Some things are like stock images: I'll be shown a white rose to indicate congratulations for an upcoming birthday or celebration. A red rose marks an anniversary of a wedding or death. Parallel lines indicate there's a parallel between the spirit and the person I am reading or, depending on the context, someone else. For instance, if they look alike, have the same name, or share some similarity or interest.

Some images are easy to interpret. I have been shown Mickey Mouse to indicate there was a trip to Disneyworld. A badge might symbolize something to do with law enforcement. Diseases are even more literal. If I'm shown blood circulating through a body, for instance, it usually means the person passed of a blood disorder such as leukemia or AIDS, or, depending on what else I'm getting, that the person sitting in front of me has such a disease affecting the bloodstream. Black spots on a part of the body indicate cancer.

Because errors in interpretation are the most common problem in readings, I sometimes try too hard to get it right and wind up overinterpreting. As the saying goes, sometimes a cigar is just a cigar. During one reading, a woman's husband came through strong and clear. He gave me many details that his widow confirmed as accurate. The reading was like a gift; I felt like I was hardly working. But throughout the session, I kept getting an image whose meaning I couldn't pin down. It was a bell. What could this mean? I started throwing out possibilities to my client: Liberty Bell, Philadelphia, Ben Franklin, Betsy Ross, Colonial America. The woman kept shaking her head and saying no. Finally, almost in desperation, I said, "He's showing me a bell. Do you know what he means?" She froze and gasped. I saw tears forming. She took a deep breath and told me that her husband had gone on a business trip and brought home a souvenir bell but had forgotten to give it to her when he came home. Getting ready for work the following Monday morning, he saw the bell in his briefcase, walked back into the bedroom, and rang it. "If you ever need me, ring this and I'll be there," he said with a smile. He put the bell on the night table and kissed his wife good-bye. He was killed in an accident on the way to work. Sometimes a bell means . . . a bell.

Spirits love to show me numbers. Barely a reading goes by without my seeing at least a couple, though their meaning is often vague. If I'm shown the number 7, for instance, it could mean something significant happened in July, the seventh month, or on the seventh of a month. Or even that it happened seven months ago or seven years ago. And there are times when it's not clear what that significant event is. It could be a birth. It could be a death. So the number will only be a small piece in the puzzle: it only has meaning when put together with other information.

In many cases, spirits will show me things I will relate to but which are meant to represent something else to the person I'm reading. For instance, I'm often shown my own car. It might mean that the spirit passed over in a car accident. It might mean he sold cars for a living. It might mean that the person I'm reading is now driving the car of the person who has passed. I often need the client to help me pin this down.

Spirits give me messages in part by knowing what I will understand. Their genius is in using a combination of human logic and spiritual energy to put the right images in my head. It's as if they're saying, "How can we get him to say this?" My brain is their file cabinet, and my life experiences are the files and folders inside that cabinet. Or to give it a more modern analogy, it's as if the spirits have a personal computer on which they can type in a message they want to convey and up on their screen will pop the best way to get that message across. For me, pop culture references are common: TV shows, movies, Broadway shows. Shelley Peck once told me, "John, I wish I knew as much TV as you do. It would make it so much easier."

But then, sometimes it just complicates matters, especially if I try to interpret information rather than telling a client exactly what I'm being shown. One tough night, I kept telling a woman who had lost her husband that "Kim" or "Kimberly" was being acknowledged. I based this on the spirit showing me Kim Zimmer, an actress who plays a character on the soap opera *Guiding Light*. But he wasn't acknowledging anyone named Kim at all. He was trying to show me how he had died. He showed me Kim Zimmer's character jumping off a bridge. This was how he had died.

This is what can happen when a spirit is not adept at communicating or a medium is not clear about what he is receiving. It can be an extremely frustrating experience for all concerned. It's why I stress that not every reading yields solid, detailed information that leaves a client floating on air. It can be vague, confusing, and disappointing.

In a good reading, I will get images that are specific to a person or a family, and are meant more literally. I once had a spirit come through showing me a bowl of spaghetti with raisins in it. It's all the confirmation her daughter needed. That's how her mother made spaghetti, every Sunday. How many people put raisins on spaghetti? No one in my Italian family.

Sometimes I know exactly what the spirit means, other times I have no clue—and neither does my client. In one reading, a woman's father came through and showed himself to me all decked out in golf apparel. "Your dad was an avid golfer, right?" I said. She told me her father never golfed a day in his life. "Really?" I said, and told her what I was seeing. "It's not my father," she insisted. But as the reading continued, he sprinkled in all kinds of golf images: a golf course, golf club, golf balls, a golf cart, even a tee. The woman said it meant nothing to her, though enough other information came through for her to feel satisfied and thankful at the end of the reading.

"I only wish he had come through with one special thing," she said as we were finishing up. "Can I ask him a question?"

"You can try," I said. "I can't guarantee he'll answer it."

"My dad used to sign things with a number. Can you ask him to tell me that number?"

I wasn't comfortable with that request. It made me feel like I was getting into some kind of numbers guessing game. As I explained this, her father showed me the golf symbolism again. "I see him swinging a golf club and yelling . . . What's that thing they yell in golf?" And I looked at her and said, "The number is four, isn't it." And she smiled. Why didn't he simply show me a four earlier in the reading? Maybe he knew I would confuse it with a month or day, though presumably his daughter would have picked up on his intended meaning if I told her I was seeing the number 4. Maybe he was trying to give me the number in an unusual, dramatic way so it would have more impact. As I said, they're in charge. And clairvoyance is often anything but clear.

Clairsentience is the hardest to describe because it's more a *feeling* than anything else. I'm not seeing or hearing it, but it's around me, as if I'm somehow *wearing* the feeling. Unlike with the other senses, it also tends to hang around, rather than whizzing by me. And if I'm not getting it right, the feeling will start to feel bigger and bigger until I do. In that sense, it is a living, breathing experience, with spirits responding to me, trying as hard as I am to bring the messages through.

Clairsentience often takes the form of an attempt to put me into the body a spirit had before passing to the Other Side, literally making me feel something of what they felt, giving me information that will validate their presence. A feeling of being hit over the head would indicate a blunt trauma, either in an accident or a homicide. A pain in the stomach might indicate stomach cancer. Other feelings are more subtle. A suicide will come through to me with the feeling that a person brought about his own death. But this is tricky ground because I will get a similar feeling for someone who caused his own death unintentionally. (Obviously, I have to be careful when conveying this to clients.)

Emotional feelings can be even more overwhelming. Later you will read about the spirit of a teenage boy whose parents were having a terrible time coping with his death and the unending sense of sadness that engulfed their house. To get my attention—and to get me to take an action that he knew would help lift them out of their grief—he made me feel what they were feeling: just *terrible*. I wanted to cry. And I was on my honeymoon.

But that is far from the norm. More often, I am given feelings of peace and love, because that is the most important thing they are trying to get across. Many times this happens in cases where a sense of guilt is involved. For instance, when a client feels guilty about not having taken an action he or she thinks might have saved the life of a loved one. Or guilt that he never said good-bye or made peace or said, "I love you." In cases like this, a spirit will often give me a feeling of great release, as if I'm suddenly let go from something. I interpret this to mean that the spirit wants me to say to the person, "Don't feel guilty. I'm okay."

On occasion, I have also been imbued with extraordinarily strong feelings of love. In these cases, which are unfortunately not that common, spirits have conveyed their love for someone I am reading by making *me* feel love for that person—someone I have never met before and will probably never see again. It comes out of nowhere. I'll be in the middle of saying something, then I start to feel a warm sensation come over me. It's as if I am at the shore, submerged in about a foot of water, and warm waves are washing over me. That spirits can seemingly get inside our brains and bodies and superimpose such images, thoughts, and feelings is the magic of the spirit world. It is as hard to rationalize as it is to explain a sunset.

Some mediums use what's known as a "gatekeeper" to funnel information. A spirit guide gathers the information from all the others and passes them on to the medium. I don't work that way. My guides are there to assist—they might jump in to help, saying, in effect,

"Now show him this, tell him that"—but the information is coming from the spirits of those on the Other Side trying to connect with their loved ones. It makes each reading unique.

Is there a correlation between the way spirits come through and their personalities when they were in physical bodies? Sometimes, but not necessarily. Just when I thought I had pinned down some rules of thumb, I've had spirits who were extremely quiet in physical life come through as chatterboxes. Or the opposite. I've wondered whether people who have passed recently will come through more strongly than those who have been on the Other Side longer and so are presumably more distant. But that hasn't held true either.

I like to think of psychic energy as akin to radio waves. Even without the radio on, the air is filled with invisible signals from countless radio stations operating on their various frequencies. All you have to do to receive them is to flick the radio on and tune the dial. When I do a reading, I flick on my own switch and wait for the program to come on. And if I miss a message, they have been known to turn up the volume.

The frustration, especially in cases where obscure information flashes by quickly, is that my client can't see what I'm seeing or hear what I'm hearing. Here's some science fiction: Maybe someday there will be some kind of psychic virtual reality, where I could hook myself up to a screen and a pair of speakers, describe what I'm receiving and have the client see and hear it at the same time, maybe even feel it, especially the overwhelming feeling of love that I get. That's my dream, but until then, we'll have to settle for this less than perfect system.

Images, thoughts, feelings, sounds. To illustrate, I will tell you about a reading I did one night for a group of ten people. They arrived shortly before 7, pulling up in a caravan of cars and trooping quietly and anxiously into my living room. Their ages ranged from twenty to sixty, perhaps two or three generations of a family. Joining them was a journalist I had invited to sit in.

Groups are interesting because they add another dimension to my work. That is, putting the right spirit with the right person. At the start, the journalist, Ted, jokingly asked, "Do you think any spirits will come through for me? Or will they know I'm not a paying customer, I'm just here as an observer?" I told him, "If you're here, you're part of this."

When I do group readings or lectures, the spirits come randomly, often sending me from one end of the room to the other. I have developed a pretty good sense of where to go with them. Sometimes, they take me right to the person. Other times, when a lot of spirits are in the air at a lecture in a large meeting room, I might be drawn only to a general area, the first few rows on the right, for instance. But one thing that is consistent in these situations is that the spirits come at will, almost chaotically, as if they are an unruly mob of reporters at a presidential press conference.

But this time was different: the information came through in an extraordinarily orderly way. The group was sitting in a semicircle on a sectional sofa, and the first piece of information that came through was directed at a young woman on the extreme right side. Her brother came through with specific information, including the fact that she had recently had a baby and that the baby's sonogram was displayed on her refrigerator. As more information came through, it was directed at one person after another, in almost perfect order, right to left. This had to be the most polite and orderly group of spirits I had ever encountered.

As the reading unfolded, it became evident that the group had come in the hope of connecting with the same person: a young man who told me clairaudiently that his name was Michael As I worked my way around the room, I realized that his mother, his girlfriend, and three of his siblings had come to connect with him. Michael told me that he was in his twenties when he died, and that he had crossed over in the past year. When I got to Michael's brother-in-law, the spirit showed me my car, throwing me off momentarily. I thought it meant that he had died in a car accident. Instead, his brother-in-law said that he was now driving Michael's car.

I began getting vague images, along with a feeling of mystery. He showed me the number 2, and gave me the sense that he did not die alone, that there were two people involved. Several people nodded their heads. I also got a feeling that they had done something to bring about their own deaths. "Was this a suicide?" I asked, trying to interpret the two messages into one. "Like a double suicide?" No, they said. I was perplexed and surrounded by the feeling that I was *supposed* to feel perplexed in order to convey a feeling. That in itself would help validate Michael's presence. "I feel like there's a mystery around this," I said. Again, they nodded yes.

Now I felt drawn into the mystery, as if the manner of death was a big part of why they were here, and they wanted answers from Michael. But Michael wasn't talking. I asked him to tell me how he died. He gave me a feeling of being hit in the head or the neck. Some sort of trauma. "Did something like this have to do with his passing?" I asked the group. "Well, we don't know," said his sister. "We don't really know how he died."

I thought this was odd. How could they not know how he died? Without telling the group, I communicated to Michael that he had to give me more, that he had to come through more explicitly for his family's sake. *They need to know it's you. You have to give me more.* And with that, he responded like a tidal wave, giving me a quick series of images that I related just as quickly to the group.

First, Michael showed me water. "A large body of water," I said. "It feels like out toward the east end of Long Island." The group began to stir. "Now he's showing me water skis," I continued, as if doing a play-by-play of the action. "No. Wait." It wasn't water skis. He was showing me a Jet Ski. "This was a Jet Ski accident," I blurted.

There was a collective gasp. Yes, they said, that's exactly how Michael died. He was Jet Skiing with a friend in the ocean off the eastern end of Long Island. There was, in fact, a mystery that had not been solved. The bodies had been found, along with the Jet Skis, but the true cause of death had remained undetermined.

But Michael wasn't finished. The very next image he showed me was of myself, on the same couch his family was sitting on now. It was like watching a movie of myself. The scene was from real life. It was the previous summer, and I was sitting on the couch watching a news report of this accident. A woman with a foreign accent was being interviewed. She was the mother of a young woman, the other victim of the Jet Ski accident. And as I watched myself watching the news report, I remembered thinking that I had known that day that these people were going to come to me for a reading.

I told the group what I was seeing. "I'm sitting right where you're all sitting, watching this on TV, and my guides are telling me, 'This man's family is going to come for a reading some day.' This was last summer, right? This is what he was showing me." Michael's family confirmed that the other victim's mother was Italian and spoke with an accent. And she was interviewed on television. The accident had occurred eight months before.

This was a turning point in the reading. After that, Michael seemed to open up, coming through in ways that allowed me to describe his personality, the kind of information I usually get only from spirits that aren't holding back. Through clairsentience, he let me know he was somewhat cocky, and a little bit vain—a not-a-hair-out-of-place kind of guy. When I said he was showing me sunglasses, his family all smiled. Now *that* was Michael, always with the sunglasses. I continued working my way around the half-circle, and when I got to Michael's girlfriend he gave me a feeling that it had been a rocky relationship. "He says you should not make the same mistakes in your next relationship that you and he made," I told her. The young woman struggled to hold back tears. "He says to tell you he knows you have the ring in your purse." At this, she began to cry. She put her hand in the purse and pulled out the ring he had given her.

Michael never told us exactly what caused his death—although the feeling of the force to the head or neck might have been a clue—but to his family, the main message was that he was all right. He came through out of love, and wanted them to know that whatever the cause of the accident, he was okay now.

Remember Ted, the journalist? After I had made my way around the group, connecting them with several other spirits, a distinctly new spirit announced himself. "Someone is here who hanged himself," I said. For the first time all night, I had no clue where to direct the information. I panned the group, as if to say, "Hanging? Anyone know someone who hanged himself?" Nobody volunteered. When I got to Ted, I felt a possible connection. "You?" I said. Up to that point, he was the only one in the room I hadn't given at least some information. "Well, no," he said self-consciously. "I mean, I was thinking of someone, but it's a very tenuous connection. It's nobody I'm related to, or even met . . ."

"Initial L?" I answered quickly, cutting him off.

"Well, yes," Ted said softly, his scoffing tone suddenly replaced by a startled nervousness. "Last name begins with 'L.' "

"I'm getting the sense that it was in a dark place," I said. "He's showing me bottles of wine, like it's a wine cellar."

"This person did it in a basement. I don't know if it was a wine cellar."

That was all I got. But later, after the group had left, Ted stayed to discuss the evening. He asked me how I'd gotten the Jet Ski accident and some other questions, but what he really wanted to talk about was the person with the initial "L" who had hanged himself. He explained that he was writing a book, a true story about a serial killer, and that there was a peripheral figure in it who had hanged himself back in 1965. "When you said hanging, I thought of him because I was just writing about him," Ted said. "But I didn't really think it was him because he's really not connected to me. Although I *have* gotten to know his widow, who plays an important part in the main story of the book."

"Well, if it was him, that may be why he came through," I said. "Maybe he's trying to get a message to his wife."

"I'd love to know if it was him. Did you get anything more about him?"

At this, I was shown a white coat with a Red Cross symbol. "Doctor," I said spontaneously. "Whoa," Ted said. "He was a doctor. Keep going." I tried. But there was nothing more. A little while later, however, I went upstairs to get an old paperback copy of Ruth

Montgomery's *Herald of the New Age* to give to Ted. As I came down the stairs, he looked up and asked again, "I'm really intrigued by that hanging thing. Did you get *anything* more on that?" As soon as the words came out of his mouth, I said, "Sy," a direct response that went through me so quickly that it was almost as if it wasn't me who was responding. Ted looked startled. "He had a cousin Sy," he said. "It sounds ridiculously obscure, but it's one of the few things I know about him. In the book, I tell a story about him and his cousin Sy."

"That's what they do," I explained. "They give information that may be so specific and obscure that it's their way of validating themselves. In this case, this guy probably knew that his cousin's name would be one of the few things you would recognize as validation. And you saw how quickly I responded."

I saw Ted a few months later, and he said he'd been thinking about our earlier encounter a lot, and was trying to decide whether or not he was a believer. "One thing I've been wondering about is how you distinguish these spirit messages from your own thoughts," he said. "I mean, if they're like voices or thoughts that flash through your head, how do you know it's not your own mind at work? For instance, at that group reading I sat in on . . ."

He began to recap the story of the doctor who had hanged himself. I shrugged in ignorance, unable to recall anything he was telling me. "I never remember much," I explained, "because they're not my thoughts. And I see a lot of people. I'm just the messenger. So I remember you were there, and I do remember the thing with the Jet Skis because it was so unusual, a really good reading, but not much else."

"Well, after everyone left," he reminded me, "I was telling you there was a man in the book I'm working on who hanged himself, and you said, 'Doctor.' Now, I had already told you that the book had a medical aspect to it, so I wonder if maybe there was a kind of synapse that made you think, 'Doctor.' I mean, how do you know it was a spirit message, and not your own thought, maybe one of those involuntary, subconscious associations we all make sometimes?"

"They're telling me 'Earl,' " I said without hesitation—a spirit message that answered his question better than any mushy explanation I could have come up with, for it seemed a chill went down Ted's spine as he told me that I had just given him the confirmation he had been holding out for. He had never told me the doctor's name. It was Earl Loggins.

Ted took a deep breath. "John," he said, "what just happened? What did you hear?"

"You asked me that question," I explained, "and I heard, *Tell him Earl.*"

"Was that him, do you think?" Ted asked. "Was that Earl Loggins?"

"No," I said. "It might have been him that other time, but this time it was my guides. They want you to know this is real."

THEY'RE IN CHARGE
(PART 1)

I went into a hotel meeting room to deliver a lecture one Thursday night in
February, and announced that I was putting
off my usual opening to describe what had
happened to me that morning. I was hoping
it would make sense to one of the three hundred people sitting in front of me. "I'm going to tell you exactly what happened and
how it unfolded," I said, "because someone
wants to connect with one of you and I'm
going to have to do some psychic detective
work with your help. I don't normally do
this, but I have been walking around with
this energy all day and I have a strong sus-
picion it is meant for someone here tonight.

"This morning," I told the group, "I had
just come out of the post office and was getting ready to start the car and go home
when I thought, *I've got a lot of people
coming tonight,* and asked my guides to
help it go well. *Please make sure everybody
understands what I'm saying, and please let
the spirits come through loud and clear.* At

that instant, I had an overwhelming feeling to drive out to eastern Long Island—specifically to an outdoor shrine called Our Lady of the Island. I know this may sound like I'm a nut, but it was so powerful that I didn't question it for a second. I just drove.

"I got there an hour later, and as I got out of my car I was told to go to the last bench. I'm thinking, *Okay, I'll go to the last bench.* But I see that there are dozens of benches, all in a semicircle. Which one's the last bench? *Right up the middle,* I was told. So I started walking straight up the middle and plopped myself down on what I considered the last bench. Now what? Someone started to come through very clearly. There was a young man who was telling me that something very specific is happening today or tomorrow or maybe later in the week—I'm hoping this will connect with your energy and make it easier to deliver this message. He was talking about a birthday or an anniversary, and then he said to me, *Michael.* Now believe it or not I'm very skeptical when it comes to stuff like this. I'm standing here telling you I talk to dead people, but I know that in order for me to convince you that I can do that, I really have to have some sort of proof. So I said, *C'mon guys, you're gonna have to help me out here. I've driven fifty miles and I need some information.*

"At that, I heard, *Look down.* I did, and saw a name inscribed on the bench: 'Michael.' I sat down and looked around. There was a tree nearby, and a pinecone dropped out of it. I picked it up. *So what am I supposed to do with this?* At that instant I was shown a box with a ribbon on it, indicating a gift. Was I supposed to give this pinecone to someone?"

Now, I asked the group, "Is there a Rose in the audience? Whoever this is has been showing me roses all day." A woman in the back raised her hand. "Rose, is there a Michael connected to you who has crossed?" Rose said no. "Well, this energy has been with me all day," I continued, "so please bear with me. He claims to be someone's son and he's giving me the name Michael. And I'm getting Rose. I feel like he is with a father figure, and there is something about this period of time, a birthday or anniversary. Does anyone have a birthday to-day, or one coming up tomorrow?"

Another woman stood up and said her birthday was tomorrow. "Is there a Michael around you who has passed?" I asked. "My son," she said. "Okay," I said, feeling that I might be in the right place: birthday tomorrow, son Michael. But there was no Rose connected to him, she said. I put that aside for a moment. "Okay, now there's an indication that there's a male figure who's with Michael."

"My husband just passed away," the woman said.

"That would be Michael's father?" I said.

"Yes."

"Now, are you sure there's no Rose connected to you? Because he's been showing me roses all day."

"I put roses on my husband's grave this week, for Valentine's Day."

"Okay. Now who is Carol or Karen? Who's the hard 'C' sound?"

"I'm Carol," she said.

I felt a rush of confirmation. "What were you doing this morning?"

"As a matter of fact, I was looking at my husband's picture."

"And were you telling him, 'Tonight I'm going to this guy'?"

"Yes."

"Well, he definitely wants you to know he's okay," I told her. "He's telling me your son was there to greet him. Did he pass after your son?"

"Yes."

"He's also telling me there's a male figure to his side—could be a brother, brother-in-law, cousin, friend—who has passed. Do you understand that?"

"My brother passed right after my husband."

"Who passed around Christmas? A 'J' or 'G' sound."

"My brother John."

It was another example of how spirits are not always thinking of the most convenient way to get their messages across. One or more of these spirits felt so strongly about connecting with Carol that they felt no compunction about sending me fifty miles to see a bench with the name "Michael" inscribed on it. As I said: They're in charge.

As for the pinecone, I took the gift box symbol literally, and brought it back with me. I gave it to Carol.

I tell this story to illustrate one of the main principles of my work: spirits come through when they want, where they want, and how they want. Sometimes it is so illogical that it leaves me scratching my head. I wonder if they have a sense of drama, or a sense of humor. Why didn't Michael simply wait until that night and come through with information in the "normal" way? I tend to think he wanted to make sure that he got my attention and kept it, to ensure that I got his message to his mother.

There have been many times when spirits seem to have gone to great lengths to stand out in a crowd. This happens especially when I am appearing before a large group, and the spirits that get through tend to be the ones that are the loudest—the ones that refuse to be ignored. If a spirit wants to reach someone in that group, it has to be more persistent than the others, because what often happens in a situation like that is that I am bombarded with many different messages all at once. My ears will literally become red as I open myself to these energies and try to separate them, focusing on one at a time.

Working a crowd often puts me through my paces. A crowd of spirits, that is—a crowd of people is a piece of cake in comparison. I recall one lecture attended by about 200 people whose spirit partners were sending me all around the room, back and forth, this way and that. It felt like they were all calling out at once, and I had to do something to restore some order. *One at a time,* I said to them in my head. *Start over again and tell me who's who, who belongs where, and what's going on.*

It turned out that there were numerous members of an extended family sitting in different parts of the room, which made for quite a confusing evening. It took a few minutes to straighten out, but eventually it all made sense. One part of my ability that I would hate to do without is being able to follow their lead to the right place. I am almost physically pulled to an area in a situation like that.

In another instance, while trying to deliver some information in the back of a lecture room filled with about 750 people, I realized I was with the wrong person. I turned and walked all the way up to the front of the room, right up to a man and said, "Sir, this is for you. You have a daughter on the Other Side?" "Yes," he said. "And she was very young when she passed. And she looked just like Shirley Temple." The man began to cry.

In cases like that, being drawn to a person feels like I'm a tracking device like a Geiger counter: Tick . . . tick, tick, tick-tick-tick. But it's rarely as strong as in the previous case. More often, I'm pulled to an area, not all the way to an individual. But then again, I'm just the Federal Express man. Sometimes it takes a while for the recipient to come to the door and sign for the package.

One night, I was lecturing at a hotel and had to be done by 11:15. The hotel needed the room for a late-night event. But at nearly the witching hour, the spirit of a young person who had died in a vehicle accident came through, wanting to talk to his mom. I gave the information as it came, unsure where in the room his mother might be. Nobody acknowledged the information, even as I kept giving more details. This went on for a couple of minutes, still with no response in the audience. But he wasn't letting go, and neither could I. Then, I felt it was centered in the first half a dozen rows, on the right.

It was 11:15. "At this point," I announced, "I'd like to say to everyone on this side of the room"—I was pointing to the left—"and to everyone on that side of the room from the sixth row back: thank you for coming and please drive home safely. This side of the room, these five rows are staying. No one is leaving until we find out who this kid is. He's insisting I get this message through. And he's not coming home with me."

Not a single person in the room left. Now, the spirit took me into the second row. "It's right here," I said. "He's telling me I'm right here. Why are you guys not acknowledging this?" Now, he started showing me Avon products. "Who here sells Avon?" I asked. "Or makeup." I was right in front of a woman who seemed connected somehow. Finally, she said she sold Esteé Lauder products. "Who are you?" I asked. "Well, I'm just a friend," she said. "Why are you not acknowledging this?" I asked. "Well, his family is here," she said. "Where's his family?" I asked. She pointed to two women, a mother and daughter.

I went over to the older woman. "Why aren't you acknowledging your son?" I asked.

"Because you haven't told me it's him. You haven't said anything that makes sense."

"Are you saying your son didn't die in a vehicle accident?"

"No," she said. "He didn't."

Her son reiterated the vehicle impact feeling. "You're saying no. He's saying yes. I'll bet you he's right. You're telling me he didn't die from a vehicle impact?"

"Well, kind of."

"Kind of?"

"It wasn't a vehicle. It was a train."

In her mind, a vehicle is something with wheels that goes on a road. And she was not going to accept the information until I said it was a train. But her son was not going away until I got to her and made that connection.

I delivered the message. Now, everybody could go home.

One night I was doing a private reading for a woman when the spirit of a close friend of hers came through by name and other identifying details. Then the spirit gave me a "female figure above" feeling and showed me a telephone. The way it came through made me believe she was telling me she wanted me to actually call her mother—right then—to tell her she was fine. Normally I would not have considered doing something so audacious, but the feeling I got was so clear and strong that I decided there was no choice. I asked my client to make the call.

A bit nervously, she dialed the number and began explaining the situation to her friend's mother. Then she handed me the phone. As gently as possible, I explained who I was and why I was calling. "I want you to know I'm not nuts, and I apologize for calling out of the blue like this, but your daughter insisted I call you right now." With that, I heard the woman gasp, shriek, cry, and then drop the phone. After a few seconds another woman got on and starting cursing at me: "How dare you, you sick so-and-so." Every four-letter word in the book. I felt terrible. I thought I was going to get sued, or arrested for harassment. But the next day my client called me and said she found out what had happened. It seems that her friend's mother had been reading *We Don't Die*, the bestselling book about medium George Anderson, by Patricia Romanowski and Joel Martin. She was so persuaded that spirits seemed to be able to practically make phone calls to those they left behind that she asked, "Why can't my daughter call me?" A few seconds later, the phone rang. She picked it up and heard a stranger saying he was a medium and that her daughter insisted he call.

This brings me to an interesting question someone once asked me about the "needs" of spirits—in short, do they have the same kinds of emotional needs they had when they were here? This person's grandfather had just come through, twenty years after he passed, and she wanted to know if that meant that he had "just been sitting around waiting to get through to me for twenty years." And if so, hadn't that been frustrating for him?

The answer is twofold. First, I believe that spirits do have an emotional side that is attached to who they were on this side. But they are straddling two worlds. And this is the second thing to keep in mind: They are *spirits* living in the spirit world, which means that their emotions are tempered by the happiness of being there. So while they know that we are hurting deeply over their physical absence, they also know that they are in a wonderful place. Our yearnings are different. We yearn to make that emotional connection to them one more time, while they're most interested in assuring us that they are all right, because they know this is really what we need to hear most.

So back to the question: Was that woman's grandfather frustrated by waiting twenty years for her to come to me? No. I don't think spirits get frustrated in the human sense because time as we know it has no meaning to them. What he probably did was to come through in other ways: dreams, feelings, signs. He may have even had something to do with her coming to me. As shown in many examples in this book, spirits have a way of getting their messages through, and in some cases this means arranging an encounter with a medium. But it's also important to remember that while I may take some of the subtlety out of it and bring messages through more directly, it doesn't mean I'm the only way through. That's why I'm always trying to get people to open their minds to what they may be missing.

After-death communication now has a solid body of evidence behind it. I hear many stories from people I encounter at readings and lectures, some quite compelling. One woman, Janet, told of window-shopping at a jewelry store in a mall. She spotted a necklace and thought about how much her mother would have liked it. Just then, someone, a total stranger, came out of the store and walked up to her. "You look like you could use a hug," the woman told Janet, then threw her arms around her. Then, without another word, she went back into the store. When Janet went back to the store the following week to talk to the woman, nobody knew who she was talking about. Hundreds of stories of after-death communication can be found in two books, *Hello from Heaven!*, by Bill and Judy Guggenheim, and *Love beyond Life*, by Patricia Romanowski and Joel Martin. Says Judy: "After-death communications—ADCs—are spiritual gifts, intended to reignite our spiritual awareness of who we are and why we're here, and our awareness that there is no death, and that we have a love for another that is eternal."

Are after-death communications successfully brought about because spirits live on a plane so timeless that knowing the future—an idea that is positively amazing to those of us on this side—is a matter of course to them? And can they manipulate events? Here's a story that suggests just that.

At the end of a group lecture in New Jersey attended by approximately 350 people, someone kept coming through to me in a very specific, explicit way. He showed me a large hand with a coin in it—either a dime or a quarter—that had been put in his hand just before his casket was closed. This image was accompanied by a feeling that the coin was for a telephone call. I asked if this made sense to anyone, and a woman I had read earlier in the evening raised her hand. Her name was Louise. "This may be a close friend of my husband's," she said. "His name was Richie." Louise's husband thought someone had done something like this at Richie's wake. But they didn't know anything more, and we left it at that.

As often happens, I heard the rest of the story soon afterward. A friend of Louise's got in touch with me and said that after the lecture, Louise and her husband had gone out to a favorite restaurant for a bite to eat. But the place was packed, and they decided to go to another restaurant. There, who walks in but Richie's brother and sister-in-law. Louise went up to them, explained the situation, and asked, "Did you put anything in Richie's casket?" Richie's brother said yes: "A can of beer, a newspaper, and a quarter so he could call us from heaven and say he was okay. I told him to call me when he got there."

Richie, obviously, wanted to make that call, and when his best friend and his wife showed up at the reading, he saw a way. But how did he know they were going to encounter his brother later that night? Did he have anything to do with it—for example, getting them to go to the second restaurant? These are part of the mysteries of the Other Side.

This was far from the only time a spirit has communicated information relating to his official good-bye. Funerals and wakes, like the circumstances of the deaths themselves, are often the subject of spirits' most vivid messages: who was there, what happened, unusual items they were buried with. That is because the passage from this side to the Other Side is such a momentous occasion for all involved. Not only is it a deeply traumatic event for those left behind, but a rebirth for the spirit. So it's not surprising that they will reminisce, so to speak, about the ceremony marking the soul's passage to the next level of life.

In one reading, for instance, a spirit showed me a uniform and a fire, and gave me a smoky feeling. The client confirmed that her husband was a firefighter who had died on the job. "He's telling me somebody kind of like fell at the funeral. And he's making me feel almost like it's funny." She said that it was a scorching day in the middle of summer, and her husband's best friend, another fireman, nearly passed out from the heat and the emotion of the moment. But he fell into the arms of a captain, which, in the macho culture of firemen, earned him some razzing later on. That was the feeling I was getting—as if the spirit was joining in on the razzing of his buddy.

APPRECIATING THE MESSAGES

Here's Rule Number One when going for a reading with a medium: Check your expectations at the door. I've had countless people say to me after a reading things like, "That was great, but why didn't my father come through?" Or, "Why didn't my sister congratulate me on getting married?" And they'll dismiss the reading because it wasn't what they wanted to hear. The main thing I tell people is to appreciate the experience for what it is. Cherish whatever message you get. It won't be the meaning of life, but it may be a piece of it.

One episode that helped bring this idea into focus for me occurred a few years ago when I read a young woman who sat down and announced, "I know that my dad is around me. He wants to tell me something, and I know it's important. He's trying but I don't know what it is." She had come to me expecting that I would deliver the momentous message. And I bought into it: I expected her father to tell me something profound, or at least where the money was hidden.

Her father did come through, but it was typical information: some details about how he lived and died, a birthday, an illness in the family, his favorite TV show, and the assurance that he was fine on the Other Side. It was good, solid validation, but nothing like what she hoped for and fully expected, and when we were done her eyes were filled with disappointment. "Didn't the information make sense?" I asked. "Well, yeah," she said, "but why didn't you give me what my father's been trying to get across?" I said, "Well, maybe he's just been trying to show you that he's around you." She nodded, but I could see it wasn't what she wanted to hear. She was crestfallen.

As is often the case, this woman was putting her expectations on *me*. And that's missing the point, too. As a medium, I'm just the messenger. I'm the speaker. There is certainly a difference among legitimate mediums in how well the messages are delivered, but the messages do not come from me—they come from Them.

This reading clarified something I'd always known instinctively but which I now realized was an issue that had to be addressed directly. There is a mythology that has developed around the work of mediums. And one myth is that if these spirits are real—if they are speaking from a dimension with access to the true meaning of life—then they should be sharing these secrets with us. I am often asked: Why isn't the information more profound? Don't spirits have anything more important to say than something like, "She wants me to talk about the bread pudding she used to make"? My answer is that this stuff *is* important. It validates their existence. And to me, that's profound.

I look for facts, as many as possible, even if they are mundane, because they will form the foundation for what may come later. In other words, if someone sits down and I say, "Your dad's here and he sends his love and he's a lovely man and he's standing right behind you . . ." it won't have real legitimacy and meaning if I haven't come through with detailed, factual information to validate the spirit's presence. It sounds nice, but it's what I call fluff. You'll appreciate the personal message more, I tell people, if I am so clinical and factual that you can't deny it.

It's also important not to play the "He wouldn't have said that" game. A woman came to me hoping to connect with her son. He came through with some specific information, including his mother's name, Ellen. But she was unmoved because she felt that most of the things I was giving her were not what her son *would* have said. So she more or less disregarded what I was passing on from her son—until he gave me something she couldn't ignore. I got a feeling that he wanted me to make fun of her name. "I'm sorry, but did he ever call you Smellin' Ellen or something like that?" I asked. The woman looked at me, and it was obvious something finally clicked. "When I was a kid they called me Smelly Ellie," she said.

In another case, a young woman came to me hoping to connect with her fiancé, who had recently committed suicide. And he did come through, but it wasn't just love and peace. He came through talking about the jealousy and contentiousness that apparently marked their relationship. I felt bad for her, and saw that when we were done she didn't want to leave. I asked her if she wanted to talk about what she had heard.

"You focused on all the negatives," she said.

"I didn't—he did," I said. "And that's probably because it's something that's not finished between the two of you. And that's what he felt was important. Maybe so you don't repeat the same pattern with someone else."

"But he didn't tell me he loved me."

"If he didn't love you, he wouldn't have shown up in the first place. This whole thing is born of love."

I have always tried very hard to keep my ego out of this. But I want so much for my clients to have a positive and persuasive experience that admittedly, I sometimes find myself frustrated when they don't and I know it's because they're resisting, for whatever reason. On one hand, many people come to me in pain. They've just lost someone, often a child, and I have to be as delicate and patient as possible. On the other hand, I have come to feel, in a way, that the spirits are my clients as much as the people sitting in front of me are. In effect, they're going to all this trouble to put out the kind of energy necessary to come through, and I feel a responsibility to them to make those connections. And if I am hitting on specific information validating a spirit's presence, and the recipient is saying "No," then I have been known to say, "Look, I'm just the waiter. I'm not the chef. My job is to bring you the food from the kitchen. It's up to you whether you have a feast or stay hungry." However, I have on occasion also been something of a pit bull waiter, force-feeding the meal.

Some people hold out for an unreasonably high standard of proof. It's something akin to a juror who ignores all the circumstantial evidence of a crime because he just doesn't want to *believe* the defendant did it. While I don't want people to try to fit square pegs into round holes, and while I don't want them to accept generalities as validation, I do want them to understand that there is more art than science to what I do and that not all round holes are a perfect fit. Be a good juror: Be reasonable, use your common sense, and go with the preponderance of the evidence.

When I think of someone who was not using her common sense, who was missing a valid message because she was being way too literal, I think of the woman a few years ago who turned a group reading into one of the longest and most frustrating nights I have had. About forty-five minutes into this session, a male spirit pulled me to one side of the room and started giving me the feeling that I was in a burning room. I felt the heat. I announced to that side of the room that a male figure to someone's side—a husband, brother, cousin, friend, etc.—was coming through saying he had died in a fire. Everyone looked around to see who this message was meant for, but nobody said a word. Then I got the same feeling again, and repeated it to the group. Still nothing. But this spirit was determined. He kept pushing me over to one small area of the room, finally to a particular row of chairs. I repeated the information for the people in this row, but still no one acknowledged it. It seemed directed at a particular woman, but she said nobody she was connected to had died in a fire. I decided to drop it for now. I asked this spirit to step aside and let others come through.

This reading was still going at nearly one o'clock in the morning, five hours after it started, when the man from the fire started coming back through. By now there were only a few people left in the room. (During these long group sessions, I often "weed out" the group by telling people it's okay to leave after someone has come through for them.) Those remaining were scattered around the room and I asked them to come closer to the front. One of those still left was the woman I had been directed to earlier. She was now in the front row, looking tired, withdrawn, and disappointed. The spirit came back and said it was definitely her. "Listen," I said to her, "this man is coming through and telling me he is your husband and he died in a fire."

"No," she said. "My husband died in the hospital." With that, she broke down and cried. Bewildered and exhausted, I turned my back and started pacing in the opposite direction. Then, something clicked. I pivoted, turned to her, and said: "Why was he in the hospital?"

"Smoke inhalation," she said. And third-degree burns. He was in a fire. But he didn't die in the fire. He died in the hospital.

This is not to say people should accept everything without question or make things fit that don't. I want people to insist on solid confirmation, which is why I tell them to be skeptical, though not cynical. There's a big difference. Being *skeptical* means not accepting vague generalities as validation. Being *cynical* means refusing to believe the evidence. In every reading, I insist on validation myself. I don't want someone to force information into a picture. For instance, I might say, "There's a Brian coming through, and it's someone above you"—meaning the generation above, a parent, grandparent, aunt, or uncle. If my client says, "Well, my son was Brian," I will say no, this is someone *above* you. I won't let them make that easy but false connection.

I am talking here about healthy skepticism. And the reason is that in these "New Age" times, when everyone and his sister seems to be some sort of psychic, when you have these 1-900-DIAL-A-PSYCHIC lines and storefronts advertising five-dollar palm readings, it's important to be careful out there. This is not to say that I'm slamming anyone. There are some excellent psychics and mediums with exciting abilities. Some of them have become nationally known, while others are known more locally. But like everything else in modern life—whether you're buying a car or having surgery—it's important to be a careful consumer. The same applies to psychic practitioners.

There is an easy way to distinguish the legitimate people from the pretenders: Do they come through with accurate, detailed validation or is it all vague generalities? The best way to test is to be skeptical. Don't make it easy for them. Skepticism, in fact, only helps a good medium do his job because someone who is being skeptical is someone who is thinking. Every true medium wants to read for someone who's thinking about what he's saying, because that only helps him deliver the information effectively. Conversely, a thinking person is the last thing an illegitimate "psychic" wants to see.

I once had a client for whom I came through with a lot of very solid information from her son, who had passed as a child. But she was barely reacting to what I was saying, as if she was afraid to acknowledge it. After a while, I decided there was something here I didn't know about and asked her what was going on, why wasn't she reacting to what I considered an excellent reading? She told me that she had been to another medium some time before and been told that her son was in "a cold, dark, lonely place longing to be with his mother." Right away, I knew this person was a phony, and I'd have to repair the damage. I asked the woman whether the other "medium" had come through with any real information to validate that he was communicating with her son's spirit. Not really, she said. And then I pointed out all the things I'd told her in the past fifteen minutes that were on target. Did he say he was suffering? No. Did he say he was scared? No. Did he say he was lonely? No. And yet, you think your son is in a cold, dark place, longing for you. And I told her that her son was in fact in a good place, that he was fine, and that he loves her and she shouldn't worry. Because that's exactly what he was telling me.

I know firsthand how hard it can be to resist expectations. I've been read by other mediums and found I'm no different than the people who come to me. In one reading with a respected medium, I came in hoping my mother would come through. I was disappointed when all I got was my father's side of the family. There was almost nothing from my mother. But I knew it had nothing to do with the medium. It had to do with those who have passed over, including my mother. She always wanted me to be closer to my father and his side of the family. And I really believe this was her backhanded way of pulling some strings from the Other Side. She stepped aside to let my father's side of the family in.

No, I am not immune from expectations. The best example of this can be traced back to a conversation I had with my mother shortly before she passed. I came into her room and said, "Ma, we have to talk about this 'Other Side' stuff." We'd talked about it in the abstract, of course, and in relation to other people, but we had avoided what was staring us in the face. Would we be able to re-connect after she crossed over? "We've got to come up with some sort of symbol," I told her. "Something so that when you get there you can kind of like ring back and let me know that you made it there okay and that everything is all right and what I'm doing is okay." (This was apart from the white bird I later asked her to send me within minutes of her passing and which I found at her wake.)

We came up with three things—three very specific symbols which I have never revealed to anyone and won't now, for reasons I'll ex-plain in a moment. I told my mother that it would have to come through another medium for me to feel it was valid. I didn't want to have to grapple with the possibility that it was coming not from her, but from my own subconscious. It was very clear between us what these signs were to be; I even told her exactly what to show the medium, in case that medium had trouble interpreting the message. My mother was a very diligent person when she was alive so I fully expected to see these validations.

I went to other mediums, hoping to get these three symbols, or at least one or two of them. Nothing. I kept waiting. Meanwhile, in the year after my mother died, I actively blocked her from coming through to me directly, knowing I was far too emotionally involved to discern if what I was getting was the work of my desire and imagination. Reading myself is like a surgeon operating on himself.

One day a year or so after my mother died, I was driving to a seminar at a hotel in New York when I felt that my mother was trying to come through. Again, I kept her out. I turned the volume on my radio way up and started singing along. Then, my mother started showing me images of when she was sick, very attention-getting scenes that I had trouble ignoring. Finally I told her, "Don't talk to me. Talk to Shelley." Shelley Peck was going to be at the seminar.

When I got to the hotel, I saw another medium, Suzane Northrop, author of *The Séance: Healing Messages from Beyond*. I knew Suzane only casually; we had crossed paths once or twice at appearances. But as soon as she saw me, she came right up to me and said, "John, is your mother passed?" I told her she was. "Did she pass of cancer? Cancer of the chest, like lung cancer?" Yes, I told her.

"Well, my God, this woman has been yelling at me all the way here. Telling me to tell you don't you ever, ever tell her not to come through to you like that again." I could not believe what I was hearing. "Your mother says to tell you that if she wants to tell you something she'll tell you herself and not to tell her to go to somebody else."

I stood there, dumbfounded.

"All the way over here," Suzane continued, "she's telling me 'Johnny, Johnny, Johnny.' And I'm thinking, 'Who's Johnny? I have no Johnny.' Then when I came in and saw you, I knew it was you. John, you can't be telling her not to come through. You can't be sending her to someone else."

I was so stunned by the whole thing that I couldn't read any more that day, and needless to say, I have never slammed the door on my mother since then.

Why did she go to Suzane, rather than Shelley? Maybe she wanted to really get my attention by going to someone I barely knew. Or maybe she was telling me: Don't send me away—and don't tell me who to go to.

Since then, I have had several what I call visits from my mother. These are times when she has come to me while I am most able to receive her: during dreams. It was during one such visit that she spoke to me about my continued preoccupation with the signs we'd agreed upon. I was still waiting, but she said in effect, "Johnny, you couldn't put words in my mouth when I was alive. Don't do it now."

The larger message was much more important. She was telling me that spirits see the big picture, and that's why they don't always give us what we want. They will give us occasional signs to make their presence felt, but they don't want us to get so hung up on them that we forget that we are living in this life, in this world. We are here to learn lessons and to grow spiritually. But we must do that here—not there.

To illustrate this point, my spirit guides have shown me the following analogy. Think of a child whose doll's head comes off. The child becomes hysterical; it's the worst thing that's ever happened to her. But as adults, we know it's no big deal. She won't even remember it in a week, never mind ten years. We try to calm the child, try to explain that it's okay, but she's inconsolable. To the spirits, we are like the child in this analogy and they are the adults. To them, in the scheme of things it's not important, for instance, to play the parlor game of "give me a sign." They want us to know they are around. But they don't want us to make it the focus of our lives.

As I write this, it has been nearly a decade since my mother passed. In that time, I have been read by other mediums, good ones, on eight different occasions. And still (like Houdini, who apparently hasn't fulfilled his promise to come back) she has not given any of them any of the three symbols we'd agreed upon. (I'm not saying what they are to preserve their integrity. Should the information come through in the future, I would consider it valid only if I was sure nobody knew about it.)

I have wrestled with this for a long time. Why hasn't she come through with this information? One possibility is that she has tried but the information was not in the mediums' frames of reference and so they missed it. Another possibility is that she had a more important message for me: that it's not about what we want to hear. It's about what they want us to know. It was her way of educating me about my work: *Tell them not to get bogged down by expectations and tests.*

But I'm still waiting.

Delivering certain kinds of information can be awkward. But when I'm doing a reading, whatever I get, my client gets. I don't hold back, even if the messages are of a personal or potentially embarrassing nature.

The same holds true for bad news. In some cases I might cushion negative information, or couch it in a way that will minimize the chances for a negative result. For instance, if I'm seeing a car accident, accompanied by a feeling that this is something in the future, I know that I'm being shown it for a reason. I am supposed to pass on the information, maybe as a warning. But I'm careful how I present the information. I don't want the person to be so nervous that she makes an accident happen. So I might say, "Be careful driving," especially if the information coming through is vague. I'm careful about making negative predictions.

Occasionally someone will come to me

and say, "I don't want to hear anything negative." And I have to tell them, "If I hear it, you're going to hear it. If they show it to me, it's for a reason: either to prepare you, or to warn you so you can do something about it. But if there's something major-league negative and you're not supposed to know about it, they won't show it to me." I once got a call from someone whose husband died a week after I read her. "You didn't warn me," she said. I explained that I would have had I been shown that. "Not to be insensitive, but you weren't supposed to know."

In other cases, I find myself in the middle of unresolved relationships between people and spirits, and inadvertently bring through what is perceived to be painful or troubling information. I was once asked to conduct a "séance" to try to raise the spirit of a celebrity, and the organizers invited the press to cover the event. Toward the end, I felt a spirit acknowledging someone named Donald. "Is there a Donald here?" I asked.

There was a silence. Then, a soft voice came from the back. "I'm Donald." It was a reporter who had interviewed me beforehand. Now he seemed wary. He was here as a reporter, and a skeptical one at that. Now he was being drawn into the reading, and he had a very reluctant look on his face. "Donald, your father is here," I said. "He's telling me his name is Frank." He nodded his head, indicating Frank was his father's name. "He's telling me he's got a brother on the Other Side, Joe," I said. "Yes. My father's brother was Joe." I continued, "And Joe is telling me something about fishing. He used to take you fishing in the Narrows." That was the body of water separating Brooklyn from Staten Island. Donald looked very shaken up as I told him this. "That's right," he said. "My uncle used to take me out fishing in a little boat, down at the Narrows off Brooklyn."

"There's someone else here, a female figure above you. Your mother? Why's she covering her eyes? Was your mother blind?" I asked.

"No," he said. I went on, "She's covering her eyes. I don't know why." Then I got a sudden flash of understanding: the woman was covering her eyes to get me to say that she didn't see her son before she died. "She says you didn't come to see her," I said, trying to convey the feeling I was getting. I didn't realize how disturbing this was for the man to hear. I was just passing on the messages, as I always do, considering it objective, factual, validating information, not a mother's postmortem scolding.

But that's how Donald took it, I later found out. "My mother died about twenty years ago," he said. "She lived in Florida and I got a call from my brother saying she was in the hospital. I knew I should go right down there and I wanted to. But I was a freelancer then, and I had an interview scheduled, a very important interview that had taken months to arrange, for a story in a major magazine. I figured I'd do the interview, then go down to see my mother. Well, she died the next day, before I could get there. I have never told anyone about this. But I've felt terrible guilt about it for twenty years."

Should I have withheld that information? I don't think so. It is not my job to be a censor. I have come to believe that I am only given information I'm supposed to pass on. There was a reason Donald's mother gave that to me. It was to validate that it was her. And it came with a loving, forgiving feeling. But I had to live with the fact that in this case, I had only stirred up this man's feelings of guilt.

There are times when I get such strong messages about people's personal situations that I will do everything I can to get the message across. But I stop short of saying what the person should do about it. I have a rule that I will not take responsibility for anyone's actions. Free will is an important concept in this. And I never forget that I can always be wrong. What I do is full of ambiguity and inconsistency, and sometimes second guesses.

When I worked in a hospital, I became friends with a woman named Catherine. She worked in the microbiology department, and she had breast cancer. One day she said to me, "I need to ask you a question. I had surgery and my doctor's giving me a choice. I can go for chemo, or radiation, or both. They said I'm pretty clean and they think it's all taken care of. What do you think I should do?" And then she added, "I'm not asking you as a friend. I'm asking you as a psychic."

I said I couldn't answer that question. I couldn't make that kind of call. "If I make that decision," I told her, "I take on the responsibility for your actions. I'm here for you as your friend. Whatever you do, I'll support you." I paused, then said, "But if it were me, I'd go for the chemo. I'd want to know I had every chance possible. It's an opportunity put in front of you. If it were me, I'd take it."

I said that because I knew she should have the chemotherapy. I wasn't going to say, "Do it or you're going to die." I didn't know that. All I knew was that I was getting a strong feeling that she needed to throw everything at the cancer that she could, and tried to say this without telling her what to do. I just didn't want that responsibility.

Catherine decided not to have the chemotherapy, hoping the doctors were right when they said they "got it all." She was afraid of the chemotherapy, probably didn't want to lose her hair. And eventually, the cancer came back and it spread. She eventually died, at twenty-eight. And I have felt guilty ever since. Should I have been more explicit? Maybe. In her last days she said, "I should have listened to you." I didn't know what to say.

Catherine has never come through to me.

As you can imagine from that story, dealing with people I know can be unsettling. One day I was driving to a psychic seminar and almost hit a woman who was crossing the street. I saw her, swerved, and missed her. When I looked back to see if she was all right, there was nobody there. I backed up, and looked all around. Nobody. And then I thought, "She looked like Stacey Sullivan's mom."

Stacey Sullivan was a girl I went to high school with. And when I realized that the disappearing woman looked like her mother, I thought something was going on with her that I needed to look into. When I got to the hotel where the fair was being held, I called my friend Valerie, who knew Stacey better than I did. "I have a really strange question," I said. (By now, people are used to me opening conversations this way.) "What the hell is going on with Stacey Sullivan's mom?" My friend said, "Oh my God. Johnny, she just died. Just a couple of days ago. She had breast cancer."

It was her way of coming through to her daughter. The same thing happened with my godfather, Glenn. Driving near his house, I saw a woman who looked like his mother. In this case, I knew she was dead. The woman I saw had a long, heavy red coat on in the middle of summer. And then, like Stacey's mother, she was gone. I called Glenn and asked if his mother had a heavy red coat. He told me she wore it all the time.

In this work, dealing with unhappy events is something I obviously do every day. Unfortunately, many of the most tragic cases are unnatural deaths. Victims of car accidents, murders, suicides—I have brought through my share.

In one memorable reading, someone came through and let me know right away that he had died in an extremely unusual, even bizarre, way. He told me it was a suicide and that it was painful. He showed me a pickup truck, then a wooded area, indicating the spot where he had ended his life. When I saw a tree I wondered if he had hanged himself. But then he gave me a sense of his pain—thankfully, a relatively mild sense. I felt as though the skin on my arms and legs was being peeled off, and then I saw, incongruously, a cartoon of Bugs Bunny and Daffy Duck. The characters were trying to top each other and finally, Daffy set himself on fire with gasoline. I was nauseated when I realized what it meant. His family confirmed that this was how he had killed himself.

I have also brought through many murder victims, including those whose killers were either unknown or not yet apprehended. In one case, a woman came to me for a reading, and the spirit of her teenage daughter came through by name. It was obvious that's why she was here. "Jessica is telling me that she was strangled," I reported early in the reading. She showed me a series of images that revealed some key details: that her body was moved, that it was found by a dog against a fence and near a school, and without any clothing. Jessica's mother confirmed all these facts. Her body was found next to a fence in a neighbor's yard, though screams heard the night of the murder indicated she was attacked in front of her own house, which was down the street from the high school she attended. Her body was found by a police dog, and she was wearing only socks.

Throughout the reading, Jessica sent exceptionally strong messages of love and well-being—assurances to her mother and the rest of her family that despite her horrible, untimely, and tragic death, she was happy and well on the Other Side. But while her mother needed to hear this, I suspected it would take some time for it to really seep in and give her some measure of peace. It was obvious that a year after her daughter's murder she remained deeply despondent. One of the reasons was that—as Jessica told me—her killer had not been arrested. She also told me that the case wouldn't be solved anytime soon. I passed this on to her mother, and it seemed to confirm her own feelings. She said her husband was talking about taking matters into his own hands.

When we were finished, I was curious to hear the rest of this story. Jessica's mother told me her last name and said that the murder, and the fact that it hadn't been solved, had been in the local news. Posters bearing a photograph of a smiling sixteen-year-old Jessica and seeking information leading to an arrest had been posted in several communities. When she said this, something clicked.

"Now I know why she was showing me Staples—you know, the office store," I said. "From the beginning, Jessica kept showing me that store. Now I know why. I go there all the time, and they've had that poster up. I see it every time I go in there, and I've gotten such strong feelings when I see it that I've even considered getting in touch with *you*. But I'm very hesitant to do that kind of thing."

I asked Jessica's mother if she had any questions. She didn't, but her sister, who had come with her, did: Had I gotten any information about Jessica's killer during the reading? It was a question that hit a raw nerve.

I generally avoid playing the role of police psychic, primarily because of one experience that turned out badly. I was once asked to try to help identify an unknown killer, and came up with the name

Michael. The victim had an acquaintance named Michael, and though there was only tenuous evidence connecting him to the murder, my identification caused him to be considered a serious suspect. Later, however, the police realized they were looking at the wrong man, the wrong Michael. The murder had actually been committed by another Michael, this one a stranger. I felt that I had caused an innocent man to be viewed as a murderer. Thankfully, the error was discovered before any more harm was done, but it led me to turn down subsequent requests to help track down killers.

And that's why I had kept to myself one piece of information that had come through during Jessica's reading: an image of a man I felt might be the killer. I didn't want some innocent person fitting the description to be suspected. But when I was asked for help by Jessica's family—rather than the police—and saw how frustrated they were, I decided to take a chance and share what I had been shown. "She showed me a tall, slender man with very short hair and a beard," I said. "He has kind of a funny way of walking, almost a limp."

Jessica's mother and sister nodded their heads. "You've just described the main suspect," her mother said. "We all have a pretty good idea who did it, but the police say they don't have any physical evidence to tie him to it." Though I wanted to help, I was relieved I hadn't given them anything they didn't already know, anything that would make me regret giving them that information. Nearly a year later, I saw a newspaper article about the case. It was about how Jessica's killer had still not been caught.

Reading stories like these, you may wonder how I cope with being brought into people's grief on a constant basis. First, I suspect that it's not quite as bad as, say, an oncologist, who must face it firsthand, and with some responsibility for the outcome. They watch people die day after day. I have the advantage of distance. Secondly, I am encountering these passings after the fact, usually after people have gone through their worst days of sadness.

Mostly I see the positive light much more than the negative. When I bring a spirit through—even the spirit of someone who died in a horrible way—I am not dwelling on the loss and the pain. Though I feel great empathy for the anguish of the survivors who have come to me for solace, I know that the best thing I can do for them is to show them—both figuratively and literally—the other side of the story. I am bringing people the assurance that their loved ones have not really left them. They are not alone, and neither are you.

10

My friend Mark Misiano used to joke that I was "a freak." I remember once driving into Manhattan with him when I heard a song I liked and asked him to turn it up. He looked at me funny and said the radio wasn't on. "They're playing 'As We Lay,' by Shirley Murdock," I insisted. Mark said he'd show me the radio was off by turning it on. When he did, "As We Lay" came on. "Oh my God, I'm in the car with a freak!" he yelled out the window. *He's a freak!*

Kidding aside, Mark's reaction gets to the heart of what a lot of people wonder about. After the when-did-I-realize-I-was-a-psychic question, what they most often want to know is: Why me? Why am I among the relatively few people in the world who can communicate with the spirit plane? The simple answer: I have no idea. As I've said, my mother was fascinated by psychics, as was my uncle Joey. My father, meanwhile, once told me he had a lot of personal psychic experiences himself. He said my grandmother, his mother, read tea leaves. Does this mean there is some sort of genetic link to what I do?

I do believe in what you might call soul genetics. I believe that, like everyone else, I made a decision before coming into this life, this body. In my case, that decision was to do this work and help whoever I can. I didn't know until I was an adult that this was what I would do. When I was a kid, I wanted to own a deli; don't ask me why. I think I liked the idea of interacting with lots of different people every day. Later, I decided to go into the health field, and majored in health care and public administration in college. Psychic readings? A "for now" thing. One day I'd stop. Once I got a Real Job.

That was on a conscious, here-and-now level. Subconsciously, spiritually, I was destined to do what I'm doing. It goes much farther back than my birth in 1969. It goes back to what I've done, where I've been in other lifetimes. All of us inhabit a series of lives, playing different roles in our souls' journeys on the road to higher wisdom.

I like to explain this by using college as an analogy. In college you're trying to accumulate enough credits to graduate. But in order to take the courses that will give you this credit, you need to take prerequisites. I think my past lives were prerequisites for the work I'm doing now. I think I've been tapping into psychic energies for a long time, building on the experiences. I don't have memory, but my soul does. Another way to look at it is this: "Jerry Maguire" is not aware that Tom Cruise was "Top Gun." But Tom Cruise is aware that he was both, and he—like the soul—will use both experiences to improve his performance in his next role.

My first "role" after graduating from college, my first Real Job, was as a phlebotomist in a hospital. I took people's blood. Meanwhile, I continued doing readings at night and on weekends, and found that word of mouth was spreading about what I do. I'd come home to find my answering machine full of messages (from people, not spirits) and even began getting calls from out of state. As I got more calls from people interested in private readings, I started putting groups together for readings, which was a way to reach and satisfy a lot of people at once. These are also called "séances," though I no longer use that term because it conjures images of a dark, spooky room with candles. My aim is to demystify spirit communication.

I found that by giving group readings, I could demonstrate differences in spirit communication. These gatherings can number anywhere from half a dozen to forty people, and the spirits that come through to them can vary wildly in clarity and personality. Some come on like gangbusters, others are shy and timid. And while most group readings last two or three hours, they can go on much longer. I never leave a seminar room until those on the Other Side stop speaking. I once had a group reading that lasted eight hours. But regardless of how long they lasted or who came through, I found that group readings were invariably satisfying for those involved. They are usually nights of closure, relief, tears, and even some laughter.

Though I had two basically separate and distinct lives—my "normal" life as a carefree, single twenty-something working in a large hospital, and my "other" life bringing people to an upstairs room in my grandmother's house and tuning in the spirit world—it was not uncommon for the two to converge.

One day at work, an eleven-year-old girl named Barbara was brought to the hospital for heart surgery to correct a congenital defect. I remember that she was also mentally handicapped and her speech was difficult to understand. But that's not why I remember her. It was because I had an order to draw blood for preoperative tests and all day long a voice kept whispering in my ear that the blood work ordered by her surgeon was incomplete. Somebody wanted me to draw an extra vial of blood and send it to the lab for what's called a coagulation profile: tests to determine how well a patient's blood clots. The paperwork I received only ordered a standard blood chemistry, which would be normal for a young patient in for heart surgery. But I was being told very seriously and urgently that this other test needed to be done.

As the day wore on, I thought about what I should do. I dismissed the idea of talking to the doctor about it; I was careful to be discreet about my sideline, and suggesting a test be done because I was getting spirit messages didn't seem the best approach to career advancement. I could simply put in the order for the coag test myself, but that was very risky. Tampering with a doctor's lab work order would get me instantly fired if it was discovered, even if I was trying to help a patient, not hurt her. But ultimately, I felt I had no choice. I redid the order on the computer, punched in the doctor's name, and prayed I wouldn't get caught.

And then I acted like it never happened. I never even inquired about how the little girl's surgery turned out. I worried that someone would discover the changed blood-work order and put two and two together. I told myself it was just something that was part of my workday, and filed the incident away somewhere in the recesses of my brain. Soon after that, I moved into the hospital's computer department.

I was giving a lecture at a psychic fair in February of 1992 when I happened onto another event at the same hotel. It was a ballroom dance competition filled with people spinning around in skimpy little costumes and tuxedos. The place was packed and bustling with activity. A pretty young lady in a salmon-colored gown and hair tied in a bun squeezed by me on her way into the ballroom. "Excuse me," she said, passing me quickly. I looked around and thought: this looks like fun.

"Do you want to go in and look around?" somebody asked, and I went inside and watched a couple of dances. When I left a little while later, she gave me a business card for a dance studio. I said thanks, though I didn't expect to use it. I put the card in my appointment book and forgot about it.

A week or so later, I had a string of difficult readings, and ended the night worn out and frustrated. I tossed down my appointment book, and out popped the card for the dance studio. On a whim, I called and asked for some information. The woman who answered said her name was Sandra and gave me the pitch: Did I want to come in for a complimentary lesson? I had always liked to dance, but never thought I needed any lessons. But, sure, I figured, I'd come in for my free lesson, learn a couple of moves and that would be it.

"How did you hear about us?" Sandra asked.

"I got your card. I was doing a psychic fair next door."

"Oh, you're part of that crew." The hotel had made a mistake booking the rooms and the dancers weren't pleased to see their ballroom filled with psychics. But Sandra thought it was pretty interesting that I was one.

"Who's going to be my teacher?" I asked.

"Um, I am," Sandra said. I wrote her name in my appointment book, starting with a very big "S."

There were a couple of things I would find out only later. Sandra was in charge of enrolling new students, and usually assigned the complimentary lessons to other instructors. But one of them was pregnant, so she decided to take this one herself. "You know how you just do something and you don't know why?" Sandra said later. "You don't even think about it, you just do it."

I enjoyed my lesson enough to sign up for a few more. And then, one of life's turning points: A few months before, I had gotten tickets for *Les Miserables*, but every time I thought of asking someone to go, I got a feeling of *No*. I couldn't pin it down, but sensed that I'd have to give the tickets away. I thought I'd take my aunt Theresa. As I've said, I always trust my spirit guides. The Friday before the show, I went to a party at the dance studio. A rhumba version of the song *All I Ask of You*, from the Broadway show *The Phantom of the Opera* came on, and Sandra came dancing over and said, "Let's dance."

Out on the dance floor, I was doing the new box step she'd taught me, doing my turns, feeling like pretty hot stuff. I asked Sandra, "Do you know this song?" Of course, she said—it's from *Phantom*.

"You know Broadway?" I asked.

"I *love* Broadway," she said.

It was like the bells went off. *Ask her*. I was embarrassed. She was my teacher. But I had to. "I have these tickets for *Les Mis*," I said. "My aunt was supposed to go and she got sick and can't go and I have this extra ticket, so if you would like to go . . ." and blah, blah, blah. I was set for her to say she couldn't go. "Okay," she said, and smiled.

"Okay?" I stammered.

"Yeah. Okay. But I can't talk to you about it here." Any extra-curricular fraternization between teachers and students was prohibited. "I'll give you my phone number."

For years, Shelley Peck had been telling me I would marry an "S." Every time I got involved with somebody, she'd say, "Nope. It's not the "S," even if it was another "S." A couple of months before I met Sandra, Shelley had said, "Oh my God, she's close." Who's close? "The 'S.' She's near." Then she said, "You're getting involved with a celebrity. John, the 'S' is a celebrity." I thought, "Where am I going to meet a celebrity?" Shelley said, "I see lights, I see music, I see mirrors." She thought she was seeing Broadway. What she was seeing was a ballroom.

Sandra was the girl in the salmon-colored dress.

Sandra started learning about my line of work right from the beginning. We were at the counter making our next appointment, pretending we weren't dating, Sandra saying, "And your next appointment will be Thursday at 9:45"—when I said, "Who's Rose?" Sandra looked at me and said, "My grandmother."

"Is she on the Other Side?"

"Yeah."

"Who's got the weird name that sounds like Ferdinand?"

"How about Fernando?" Sandra asked.

"It's like the same name to me. It's got the same sound."

"That's my dad. Rose was his mom."

Sandra, though, didn't understand that her grandmother was actually coming through from the Other Side, acknowledging her father. She thought I was just being a psychic, picking up that she had a grandmother named Rose and a dad named Fernando. When I explained what it was, she had a few questions.

After we started dating, Sandra's parents were a little disconcerted when they heard about my work, even though Sandra told them I had a regular, normal day job. Actually, disconcerted is a polite way of putting it. They were freaked-out by it. They called me "that witch guy," a reflection of their superstitions. "They really don't understand it," Sandra told me. It wasn't that they doubted I was communicating with spirits, but that they were very worried about what that meant. Sandra's mother told her to be careful with me. "He speaks to dead people," she said. "Maybe he could become possessed. Too much work on his brain."

Her parents felt better after they met me. On my third or fourth visit, I did an impromptu reading. Sandra's maternal grandfather came through with some information, such as details of his death. "He's telling me you speak to him a lot," I told her mother. And she smiled. Good thing: This guy who spoke to dead people was going to be her son-in-law.

The day I went to pick up Sandra's engagement ring was a bittersweet, emotionally difficult moment for me. I was happy and excited, but also sad that my mother couldn't be a part of it. I had been introduced to a jeweler by a mutual friend, and when I went to his house and looked at the finished ring, I got teary-eyed. I walked back to my car and opened the ring box. The sunlight seemed to fill the car with sparkles. I held up the ring and said to my mother, "You're the first person to see this ring, and the first to know I'm getting married."

When I got home I checked the answering machine in my room: calls from clients, mostly. And one frantic message from Shelley Peck. "John, call me right away," she said, sounding annoyed. "I've got something that couldn't possibly be true." When I called her back, she said, "Your mother's been here and she won't leave me alone. She says you're getting married. She says you showed her the ring. It can't be true—you would have told me, right?" I told her she was the second person to know, and thanked her for the latest message from my mom.

Sandra and I had a long engagement—a year and a half. By the time of the wedding, I had moved out of my grandmother's house and was living on my own. Still, my grandmother insisted that I get dressed for the wedding at her house. She said my family should be with me as I prepared for this momentous day. I told her I wanted to get dressed in my house. "And don't worry," I told her. I wasn't alone: "Mom's with me." Under my tuxedo, where nobody could see, I wore my mother's necklace, with her nameplate. I took it off later in private, and not even Sandra knew I had had it on during the wedding. I hoped my mother would come through with an acknowledgment of the necklace, confirmation that she had been with me at my wedding. It took a while to get it.

About a year after we were married, Sandra asked if I would read a small group of her mother's friends. I agreed and asked Shelley to join in. We hadn't worked together in a while, and I thought it would be fun. Most of the people who came spoke Portuguese and had little grasp of English. Shelley and I gave the information and Sandra interpreted—a psychic United Nations. It turned into a long night and Shelley and I were getting a little slaphappy when she turned to me and, apropos of nothing, said, "You wore your mom's necklace the day you got married?"

Once again, it was my mother's way of letting me know she was with me, and that she knew of the private tribute I had given her. And, of course, she did it how she wanted, when she wanted—a whole year after the wedding. Maybe it was her way of saying, "You'll get those three symbols yet. Some day."

I f there's one thing I have learned in the nearly fifteen years that I have been communicating with spirits, it's that there is no end to their surprises, and consequently, no end to my journey of discovery. When I wake up in the morning, I know it's the beginning of another day when anything might happen, when I might learn something new or feel a profound sense of affirmation that, as I often say, "I'm not amazing—they are." And there are days when I make a connection or share an experience with a client that reminds me that I am not alone on this journey. We are in this together.

11

The day I met Sue Farrell was just such an experience. She was nervous and a bit skeptical when she arrived for her reading accompanied by her husband one day in 1992. Though she grew up with the traditional belief in an afterlife that included heaven and hell, Sue's attitude about psychics who said they reached the dead had been: "How dare they take advantage of people in grief with such nonsense." But recent events had begun to change her view about after-death communication. She decided to come to me after a close friend (whom she knew through the parents' support group Compassionate Friends) had a reading and recommended she make an appointment herself. "She's a credible person, and she was blown away by her reading," Sue says of her friend, whose three-year-old daughter had tragically died from raw meat infected with E-coli bacteria. As I was about to find out, Sue had her own tragedy to deal with, and her friend thought I could help.

Like many people who came to me for the first time in the years when I had a relatively low profile, Sue was visibly surprised by how young I was. She later told me her first thought was that I looked like someone who could have been one of her daughter's friends. But this seemed to relax her—hey, what could happen? I was just a kid.

We sat down and began the reading. I quickly felt the presence of a remarkably vivacious young female whose name began with the letter T. "My daughter's name was Tracy," Sue said. "I can't believe her energy," I said. "I feel like she's lighting up the whole room. She's very bubbly." Tracy showed me my new car and gave me a teasing feeling. "She's joking around, telling me she likes my new car," I told Sue. "That's her," Sue said. Tracy used the car image as a segue to how she passed. She showed me another car and gave me an impact feeling near some trees. "She's telling me she was killed in a car accident," I said. "That's right," Sue said. "It looks like it's on a parkway, near her home and near where she worked," I continued. "Yes," Sue said. "It was on the Southern State Parkway. She was on her way to work. She crashed into a tree." Tracy was only twenty-two, only a year younger than me. She had just graduated college. "I'm getting the feeling that another car was involved," I said. "Well, that's interesting," Sue replied. "The police said it was a single-car accident but they never really investigated. They said she must have swerved to avoid an animal."

The circumstances of the accident were somewhat unclear and had left Tracy's parents unsettled, questioning the police version. But Tracy wanted them to get past that—as she had. "She's telling me she doesn't want to dwell on the accident," I told them. "She's moved on. She's very accepting of it. It wasn't her fault, but there's nothing she or anybody can do about it." (Why Tracy revealed that another vehicle was involved is an interesting question, considering that she wanted her parents not to dwell on the accident. Perhaps she felt they needed to know it wasn't her fault, and that this disclosure would put them on a path that would eventually give them some peace. After the reading, Sue hired a traffic-accident engineer, who reinspected her daughter's car and found white paint from another vehicle on the bumper. Based on that and other circumstances, he surmised that Tracy had lost control after another car came into her lane.)

Now Tracy abruptly changed the subject. She showed me writing on a wall with crayons. "Did she draw on a wall when she was a kid?" I asked. "No," Sue said.

"Well, she's showing me Crayola crayons and she's putting numbers on a wall. She's writing '143.' Does that number mean anything to you? An address? A license plate?"

Sue thought for a moment, but said it didn't ring any bells. Then, suddenly, it rang one of mine. Sandra and I had come up with a code for "I love you." It was 143, signifying the number of letters in each of those words. We used it—still do—when we signed our names in notes and cards to each other. "She's using my code to tell you, 'I love you,' " I told Tracy's parents. "That's very clever. I can't believe how clear and accurate she is."

"You think that's something?" Sue replied, sounding like anything but a skeptic. "I have a story for you."

Usually, I don't like to interrupt a reading like this, but my guides were giving me an open feeling, signaling that I should listen to what Sue had to say. So I listened.

"My daughter used to coach cheerleading," she said. "And one of her little cheerleaders, who's now a senior in high school, was very close to Tracy and took her death very hard. One day, just a few months ago, this girl was at home and she heard a beeper going off. She had a beeper when she was in tenth grade—her parents gave her one, I guess it's a status thing—but she hadn't used it in a couple of years. So when she heard the beeper, she didn't think it was hers. Her beeper was on the bottom of a drawer somewhere and she figured the battery was dead by now anyway. So she called downstairs to her mom and said, 'Dad's beeper is going off.' But her mom said no, her dad had his beeper with him. So she decides to look in the bottom of the drawer. And she finds the beeper. She presses the button and sees a whole series of numbers. First was 07734, which she immediately recognized as the thing the kids do, where if you punch those numbers in and turn it upside down it spells HELLO. After that it said 112667. She knew it wasn't a phone number. So she's looking at this beeper, which hasn't beeped in two years, and she had been thinking a lot about Tracy, and about how unfair it was that she was killed. She knew Tracy's birthday was in November. She decides to look over at her dresser, where she's got the mass card from Tracy's funeral stuck in the mirror. It gives her birth date. November 26, 1967: 11-26-67, the number on the beeper. So it says, "Hello" and Tracy's birthday. She freaked. She didn't know what to do. She calls me up and says, 'Please sit down.' She can barely get the words out. She comes over with the beeper and the numbers are still there. And the battery was dead but this message was there."

We started talking about how spirits are capable of some amazing things, all to let us know that they're still with us. "I know Tracy has visited the people who have mourned over her," Sue said. "In fact, my neighbor across the street thinks Tracy saved her daughter's life from the Other Side."

This is where the encounter changed from a better-than-average reading with an engaging client to one of those experiences that affirm that there is something truly phenomenal at work here. Sue started telling me about the girl who lived across the street from her, and my guides gave me a keep-listening feeling. "This girl has a mental handicap and was also born with congenital heart disease," she said. "She's the younger sister of a girl who was extremely close to Tracy."

As Sue started talking about this girl, Tracy—still with us—began coming in with more messages. Curiously, she showed me an image of myself doing my old job, drawing blood at the hospital. Then I realized that she was specifically showing me the incident when I was guided to order an extra blood test for a young patient. I figured Tracy was showing me this incident not as a literal message, but as a parallel symbol. In other words, she was showing me something I would recognize from my own life to get me to say something of a similar or related nature that would be significant to her mother. Meanwhile, Sue continued her story. I felt like I was trying to listen to two people talk at once.

"She was going into the hospital for open heart surgery," Sue said of Tracy's friend's sister. "She went in the night before, on a Monday, and Tuesday morning she woke up shaking. Her mother asked her what the matter was and she said, 'I had a dream about Tracy. She held me and she said she's going to be with me.' Her mother says, 'Well, that's good. That means Tracy's here and she's making sure everything will be okay.' "

Just then, Tracy told me, Barbara. "Was this girl's name Barbara?" I asked Sue.

"Uh-huh," she confirmed.

"Okay, go ahead."

"So then they came for her and put her on the gurney and took her up to the operating room. The surgeon came in, and he's one of the top surgeons in pediatric cardiology at that hospital, and he's going over Barbara's chart as he's scrubbing for surgery. And all of a sudden he looks on the chart and sees that there was a blood test that he had not ordered . . ."

Oh my God, I thought.

". . . It's a test that's normally ordered only for geriatric patients, never for an eleven-year-old. So it startled him. And then he reads the results, and immediately cancels the operation. Because the test showed that her blood was not clotting like it should. Had they started cutting her she would have bled to death on the table."

I couldn't believe what I was hearing. "You said this girl was like eleven or twelve years old?" I asked with a rush of adrenaline coursing through my body.

"Right," Sue said.

"Was this at St. Peter's Hospital?"

"Uh-huh."

"Is this girl like cross-eyed and you can't understand her too well?"

"Yes."

"Oh my God, I did that! That was me!"

Sue and her husband had no idea what I was talking about. Did what? What was you?

"I was the person who drew the blood! I work at St. Peter's. I ordered that test! I didn't know why. That whole day someone was whispering in my ear. It was your daughter!"

"Oh my God," Sue said, looking as shocked as anyone I have ever read. After we both calmed down, she told me, "The doctor called the parents in and said, 'For some reason this test was given. I don't know where it came from, but thank God it was done. Your daughter's alive because of it.' So her mother comes home and tells me Tracy did it. And I'm like right, sure."

"Well, now you can tell her she was right," I said. "Did they do the surgery later?"

"Yes, they treated her with medication and rescheduled the operation."

Needless to say, this episode says all kinds of things, not only about the powers of spirits, but about connections. That Tracy orchestrated a way to intervene in an impending tragedy is fantastic enough. But she didn't stop there. She made sure there was a lesson in it by bringing her mother to me. As Sue says, "I just believe that we get hooked up with who we're supposed to and it's amazing what happens from it."

About three years later, I had another encounter with Tracy and her mother. Once again, I'll let Sue tell the story: "Every Christmas, our Compassionate Friends chapter has a program with a beautiful ceremony where we all light candles and say the name of our child. But on the same night as the program, my ten-year-old son had a big hockey game that he really wanted me to go to. I wanted to go for Tracy, but my son is here. I chose to go with my son and watch his hockey game. It was the playoffs. My friend Louise was going to Compassionate Friends. She also lost her daughter in an accident, and she was also a cheerleader. I begged her to get an extra candle and after she said her daughter's name, to say Tracy's name. I just wanted her to be represented. As a parent, the biggest thing is that your child is not erased. She said no problem. The next morning she came over with all the literature from the program and gave me the candle she had lit in Tracy's name and said the ceremony was beautiful. I felt good that it was taken care of."

A day or two later, I returned a message I had received from Sue. She had called asking for information about an upcoming lecture I was giving. When I called her back, I told her where and when and while giving her directions, I realized that Tracy was with us. "Your daughter's here," I said. "Really?" Sue said. "She's telling me you forgot her. But she's laughing, like she's not upset, she's just teasing." I didn't know what this was about, but Sue obviously did. "Well, you tell her I took care of it," she said with mock indignation.

"After I hung up," Sue recounts, "I called Louise and asked her, 'On Friday night, you did light a candle for Tracy, didn't you?' Dead silence. And she explained to me that they wouldn't give her an extra candle when she walked in because they were afraid they wouldn't have enough. But at the end there were extras so she picked one up on her way out. She never lit it and said Tracy's name but she figured I would never find out. I told her what happened, that Tracy came through teasing me about it. And Louise said, 'So Tracy's tattling on me from the Other Side.' My daughter was tattling on my best friend. That would be her total sense of humor."

Sue says Tracy has given her and her family many signs over the years. Once, while in their car soon after the accident, Tracy's baby brother, who was only in kindergarten when she died, looked up at the sky and saw a plane skywriting a heart. "Mommy, look," he said. Sue remembered that Tracy used to write letters to her brother from college, always signing with a heart. "I told him, 'That's Tracy sending you love,' " Sue says. "I didn't really think so. I was just saying it to make him feel good. He was only six years old. Then he says,

'Mom, they're writing some more.' So as a joke I said, 'Now they're going to write "Love, Tracy." I look up and he's doing a 'T.' And then an 'F.' Tracy Farrell. I ran home and took a picture of it."

How does Sue feel now, after all these experiences? "I started out very skeptical, but it absolutely puts you at peace," she says. "We've always been brought up with heaven and hell, and you never really think about it—aside from wanting to go up, not down—until something hits you close. Now I feel that the door to the Other Side has been opened just a crack by my daughter. There's no doubt in my mind that we start our lives when we die. The only thing important down here is to love and help others and be a good person.

"I was so devastated after Tracy was killed. And later my son came and sat on my lap and said, 'I want my mommy back.' And after this, I could come back and be his mommy because I do know now that Tracy is fine."

I n the years when I was learning how to balance my worldly and spiritual lives, one issue nagged me. I was questioning how my religious faith fit into my work as a medium.

On one hand, I was living in a world of spirituality every day, feeling closer to God than ever. On the other hand, I felt isolated and alienated from the Catholic church of my upbringing because of its stance on psychic phenomena and the work of mediums. While I still considered myself a Catholic with a strong religious faith, I knew that my church was strongly opposed to what I did. A priest I have come to know well puts it this way: "According to the church, there is only one medium, and that's Jesus Christ. He will tell us everything we need to know."

By my early twenties, I felt that I wasn't part of "the team"—I wanted to be part of it, but they didn't want me. Nobody told me this in so many words, but it was clear what the church thought about spirit communication. And if they told divorced people they were unwelcome, I assumed they surely didn't want me. On several occasions, while at work in the hospital, I met priests who came in as patients. It was my job to draw their blood, and as I filled the vials, I'd strike up conversations with them. Without getting into why I was asking, I'd say, "Father, let me ask you something. What do you think about psychic phenomena?" And the answer would always be the same: "Well, you know that goes against the church." People were always telling me not to worry about it—"You've got a gift from God"— but still, the implicit rejection by the church I'd grown up in troubled me. I had no intention of stopping what I was doing. Instead, I stopped going to church. But I never stopped feeling connected to God.

One day, to my shock and great discomfort, a nun came to me for a reading. Her name was Sister Veronica, and she came dressed in her habit. I tried to act nonchalant. "Have a seat right here, Sister," I said, then dashed to the next room to call Sandra at the dance studio. "Sandra, there's a nun here," I said in a near-panic. "What should I do?"

"Well, you should read her," Sandra said calmly.

"But she's a *nun*," I said.

"But she's a person first. Call me back and let me know how it goes."

I went back in and said, "Sister, I have to tell you something. I'm very nervous reading you."

"Why are you nervous?" she asked.

"Because of the church. What I do goes against what they think. According to them, I should be excommunicated."

Sister Veronica smiled. "John," she said, "God gives people all kinds of gifts. Some people are wonderful painters, some He gives beautiful voices to sing with, some become great teachers. He's given you a voice and also the ability to teach about what you do. If you don't, then *that* would be a sin."

A rebel nun, I thought. I proceeded with the reading, and it was a good one. At the end, she said, "John, would you do me a big favor? I'd like you to do a group reading at the convent." A *real* rebel. It turned out that as a pastoral care practitioner, Sister Veronica dealt with death all the time. She ran a bereavement group and felt that what I did could do a great deal of healing. I said I would be happy to come to the convent.

I had several more readings that day, but couldn't forget the first one. With a note of amusement (and relief) in my voice, as one of the later clients was leaving I regaled her about my encounter with the nun earlier in the day. "I was so nervous reading for a nun . . ." I was saying at the door as my last client for the day walked in. He was a man in his mid-thirties and told me his name was Patrick. He sat down and said, "I think I should tell you something."

"No," I said. "I don't want to know anything. I don't need to know anything about my clients. You can tell me anything you want at the end." I closed my eyes for a few seconds, then gave Patrick the first message I was receiving. "Your dad's passed," I said, knowing I was right.

"No," he said.

"No? I'm getting this absolutely clearly. I'm being told, 'father.' "

"My father's alive."

"Then it's a father-in-law."

"No."

"Stepfather?"

"No."

"Godfather or father figure?"

"No."

"I'm hearing the word father, father, father."

"I really think I should tell you something," Patrick said.

"No. Just tell me yes or no."

"Okay," he said, smiling. "Have it your way."

"You say your father's alive."

"Last time I checked, which was just before I came over here, my father was very much alive."

I thought he was playing with me—testing me—and I didn't like it a bit. I knew what I was hearing: "father." I was getting so frustrated that I was about to tell him to either acknowledge a father figure or leave. But then in a quick flash, superimposed on Patrick I saw black clothes and a white collar. I leaned back. "You're a priest," I said. He put his hands up. "I was trying to tell you that," he said, smiling.

Father Patrick Moran (who requested that I not use his real name because of the church's position on mediumship) was a parish priest who was checking me out. So many of his parishioners had been coming to me that he wanted to see if I was legitimate. "I always had an interest in psychics, even though it's not in keeping with church teachings," he said. "But I was also leery about them. I didn't want people to be deceived, given false hope, and lose their money. The church discourages people from going to psychics, but people are going to go anyway and I wanted to discourage them from going to someone I thought was a phony."

Father Patrick was persuaded that I was legitimate after several of his relatives came through at his reading, along with the spirit of the three-year-old girl whose parents had urged him to pay me a visit after she came through at their reading. His decision to seek me out would benefit us both. In the years since, Father Patrick and I have become friends, and he says that first reading, and subsequent encounters, have confirmed his belief in the positive power of psychic mediumship. As for me, it is no accident that I got a visit from a nun and a priest on the same day, at the very time that I was questioning my acceptance by the church. He was the priest I was looking to connect with: one who believed in the principles of the Catholic faith, and yet one open enough to say to me, "What you're doing is good— keep doing it, don't stop. And you are more than welcome in this church."

Father Patrick and I have had some interesting discussions about the spirit world. "I believe your gift is from God," he has told me. "Some people could say this gift is not from God. The church thinks there are only two options, Jesus Christ or the devil, but I think there are other choices. I don't believe it's from the devil, but there are other spirits, people who walk between good and evil who can give information. They're lost souls. They're not attached to either good or evil just yet. But the church doesn't want people to play with any of this. They want you to attach yourself simply to Christ. And I don't think that's bad advice because many psychics are frauds and some are people who are conjuring up spirits that are not good." But he has told me that he supports what I do because I am connecting to spirits that are only forces of good. "It reaffirms the fact that we're all connected, that the living and the dead are not separate and there's just one world," Father Patrick says. "My favorite line from scripture is John 17:11, which says, 'Father, I pray that all should be one as you and I are one.' There's a unity between heaven and earth. There's a unity between life and death."

When I first met Father Patrick, I knew that he had some psychic abilities himself, and he confirmed that he had spoken to spirits. But when I offered to help him do it better, he demurred. Knowing that it could be done was enough for him. Taking a more active role in it would put him in uncomfortable territory. "Most of my friends who are priests are against that I have any connection with psychics," he says. "They still don't understand my curiosity." After his connection to me became known through a newspaper article about me in which he was quoted, Father Patrick heard comments from people saying he was "not allowed" to believe in what I do. "How can I not believe it?" he says he told them. "I've seen it."

After his original reading—the only formal reading I have done for him—Father Patrick's family thought he was only seeing a good guesser. They changed their minds after he and I got together for dinner at his house one night about three years later. As we were eating, my guides were telling me that Patrick's "Uncle Tony" was going to cross over. I was seeing someone in his family breaking into his house to find him dead. I got the feeling it would be soon, within a couple of weeks.

Father Patrick, understandably, was terribly shaken by this vision.

"Uncle Tony" was not a blood relative, but his godfather, a very close family friend and neighbor. He told his father and brother about my premonition. His father told him not to tell his mother, then went to check on Uncle Tony. So did Patrick's brother, who is also a priest. Both found Uncle Tony fine. But a week later, after he hadn't been seen outside for a couple of days, one of Tony's neighbors, followed by Patrick's mother, did break into his house, where they found him dead, the victim of a fatal heart attack.

Looking back, the day I met Father Patrick and Sister Veronica was the day I started to feel connected to my church again. I'd had people suggest to me that I had become closer to Scientology than Catholicism. But I never wanted to change my foundation. I am Catholic. That's how I grew up. I had felt like I was a ship sailing off into the ocean. Father Patrick came to the dock and threw me a line. I'm still out there but now I'm not adrift.

By coming to me on the same day, saying the same thing to me, the priest and the nun renewed my belief that whatever the particular religion or denomination, faith in God is extremely important. It is my conviction that whatever belief system we have on this side of the spiritual divide will help determine how easily we will make the transition to the Other Side. A strong belief in God and the expectation that the next life is a beautiful, loving place will only smooth the crossing. My connection to God has never wavered, but through my friendship with Father Patrick, born that day when he came to check me out, I have felt I am still a welcome member of my "team." I can bring people together with the souls of their loved ones and still have a prayerful place to call home. And that's a great thing because prayer is such a source of spiritual energy— not only for those of us on this side, but for the spirits themselves. It's home to us all.

As for Sister Veronica, I did go to the convent to give a group reading, and also became a regular at her diocesan-sponsored bereavement groups, giving what amounted to unsanctioned group readings twice a year. I was reminded of the fine line that had to be walked when, at the beginning of one of these sessions, I said, "I'd like to thank everyone for coming here tonight to be part of this séance." Whereupon Sister Veronica, sitting next to me, gave me a hard elbow to the stomach. She leaned forward with a twinkle in her eye and said to the group, "Spiritual gathering."

One day in the summer of 1994, a woman named June Castonguay came to me for a reading. A forty-year-old mother of two, she was interested in a general psychic reading, rather than a connection with someone on the Other Side. She saw psychics somewhat regularly because, she said, she was "just into this." To me, of course, she was merely a name in an appointment book, and as she sat down I had no reason to expect anything out of the ordinary. I am psychic, but not omniscient. I had no idea that what was about to occur would teach me something important about my two worlds, about grief and recovery, and about the power of life and love. And I had no idea that it would change the lives of several people I had not yet met and become one of the most moving and memorable experiences I have ever had.

Because June said she had been to me once before, I dispensed with the usual preliminaries, but reminded her to be open but

13

skeptical. I asked to hold something of hers, and she gave me a bracelet. And then I closed my eyes, and invited the spirits connected to June to come through with their best energies. Almost from the beginning, I felt a strong presence from the Other Side. The first thing this spirit did was to call out the name Tony. It was a father figure. June said she had a friend named Tony, still on this side. But she doubted this was the Tony the spirit meant: Why would he be seen as a father figure to her? The spirit then gave me another name, Christopher. "Tony does have a son Christopher," June said. "And his other son is also named Tony." But she still had no clue who might be coming through with these names. Someone related to them?

"I'm being shown a fatal car accident," I said. "Does this mean anything to you?"

"No," June said, searching her mind. "I don't think so."

"You're sure? Think hard. Because I'm being told you were there. Like you were a witness to this accident. I'm being shown a boy on a bicycle."

Suddenly, June's eyes lit up in recognition. "Oh my God, yes!" she said. "It was just last week. I didn't actually see it, I was up the street. But there was a boy, a teenager, who was killed. He was riding a bicycle and got hit by a car."

"Well, he's here," I said. "And he's acknowledging Tony."

Stunned and a bit shaken by the unlikely connection, June explained that she and her husband had arranged to go to Tony and his wife's house the previous Friday evening, meeting there so the two couples could go out to the movies together. When they got to their friends' house, about twenty-five minutes away, June heard that a teenager on a bicycle had been hit by a car a block or two away. Tony's sons, Christopher and Tony, Jr., went down to the scene and described what had happened. June said it didn't click right away because I had first said a car accident, and she thought of it more as a bicycle accident. And she hadn't actually witnessed it, though she realized now that for the purposes of the teenager's spirit, she was close enough. She assumed, as I did, that he gave the names Tony and Christopher to help her make the connection. She wasn't at the scene, but Tony and Christopher were.

"He wants you to tell his mother and father he's all right. He's okay. This kind of thing doesn't happen very often, so it's important. You need to tell them he's on the Other Side, and he's okay. He's showing me a white rose, which means a birthday. This will validate it for his family. He's telling me Anthony, and he's saying there's a birthday coming up."

It was one of the strongest spirits I'd ever encountered. Essentially, he'd barged into this woman's reading and made himself heard above any spirits coming through for her. Through me, he was more or less pleading with her to get in touch with his family to tell them not to worry. June took it all in, but I could tell she was shaken by the reading, unsure what to do about it. Complying with this boy's request would be awkward, to say the least. "I don't even know these people," she said. "I wouldn't know what to tell them."

I knew it would be tough, but I urged June to deliver the message and sent her on her way. And that's the last I heard about the boy on the bicycle until the following winter. I wouldn't hear the entire story for another year.

Andrew Miracolo was a popular sixteen-year-old who lived with his parents, Mary and Tony, and his younger brother, fourteen-year-old Matthew, in a house on a quiet street in central Long Island. Andy was a bright and engaging teenager with scads of friends who loved him. They rarely called him Andrew, or even Andy. They used a nickname one of them had dreamed up: Androskiday, or Drosky for short. When they called his house, they'd say, "Is Drosky there?"

Andrew and his brother were very close. They played together on the high school hockey team, and celebrated when the team won the county championship in the winter of 1994. Their parents were both teachers. Mary Miracolo was a gregarious and passionate special education teacher. Tony Miracolo taught high school social studies. Several years before, Tony had converted from Catholicism to Buddhism.

His backyard was fashioned after a Japanese garden, built with his sons' help. There was a greenhouse in which he raised bonsai trees. But nothing in this happy suburban household would ever be the same after Friday, July 15, 1994. That evening, the Miracolos' lives were shattered.

"It was about 5:30," Tony recalled a few years later. "Andy wanted to ride his bike over to a friend's house. Mary and I were going out to do some shopping. We were going to Border's and then Pier One Imports. Andy's bike had a flat tire, so I went into the greenhouse to get my bike. I gave him the bike. I told him I loved him—I did that every day. And that was the last time I saw him alive."

Andy got on his father's bike, and his parents got in the car to go shopping. A half hour later, the Miracolos were in the Pier One store when Mary felt a hand on her shoulder. It was her younger son, Matthew. He was with a police officer. "My first thought was that Andrew had done something," Mary said. "But Matt said he didn't do anything wrong. He was on his bicycle, and he was hit by a car. I knew instantly that he was going to die. They didn't have to tell me. I just knew."

There was a reason Mary felt so sure. Two of her friends, fellow teachers, had lost their sons in the very same way, in accidents while on bicycles. She remembered once sitting with them on a bench outside their school at lunchtime, and saying, "This could happen to me, too." She had feared this subconsciously ever since.

Andy had been hit head-on by a car driven by a young woman who apparently didn't see him. At the hospital, where dozens of people gathered, Mary and Tony found out that Andy had suffered severe head injuries—the "worst I've ever seen," a doctor told them later. He also had serious internal injuries.

"I started to shake when they told me about his injuries," Mary says. "I knew he was going to die, and I was going up and down the halls, crying, shaking, telling people, 'Say good-bye to Andy.' I was hysterical. 'My baby, my baby's gonna die.' And I didn't stop shaking until I looked at my watch and it was a quarter to ten, and I knew he had passed to the Other Side. He was in heaven. They pronounced him dead fifteen minutes later."

Mary says that she later realized that her spirit guides had tried to prepare her for this tragedy. "It began the Christmas before," she said. "I believe my life was changing. I read *Embraced By the Light*, and the last words of that book were that we're here to love and that you have to try. I hadn't talked to my brother in ten years, and I thought, 'How can I profess to love anybody if I can't love my own brother?' And I decided to make peace with him. How it relates to Andy is that the day before he died, I had gone to the cemetery and visited my brother's little boy, who died of cancer when he was four. And when we were at the hospital with Andy, somebody asked me where I wanted him buried. I thought, What a question to ask. But I had on a fanny pack, and the only thing in it besides money was a piece of paper with the lot, block and section number of my nephew's grave. And I decided I wanted to have Andy buried there."

There was also an indication that Andy's own guides were preparing him. "A few months before he died," Tony said, "I was talking to him in his bedroom about learning to drive. I had gotten the information about the permit and the procedures, and he said, 'Dad, I won't need this. I'm never gonna drive.' I asked him what he meant— 'You're sixteen-and-a-half, you'll learn to drive.' He said, 'I'm not gonna live,' and he was very emotional. We had a big conversation about it. I said, 'Andy, we all feel at times that we're going to die.' But he was crying—he couldn't talk about emotional things without crying—and I was very shaken by this."

"Kurt Cobain had just died," Mary said, "and he liked him so we thought he was sad over that."

"But I also had a dream months before that one of my kids was going to die," Tony said. "I thought it was Matt. And I woke up crying, asking God, 'Please don't take my son.' "

Despite these precursors, of course, Mary, Tony, and Matt were inconsolable when Andy was killed. The day after he died, as scores of people streamed through their house, Mary lay across the couch in the living room, crying, screaming, almost pleading with God for some word of comfort about her son, some way to know he was in Heaven and that he was all right. "If Andy could write us a letter and tell us he's okay, he would do that," she told her husband through deep sobs. "As sensitive as he was, he wouldn't want us to go crazy like this. If he could, he'd write us a letter so we'd know he's okay."

June Castonguay was beside herself, unsure what to do. She had simply gone out to the movies with her friends on a summer night; now, four days later, she was being told by a psychic that she was supposed to contact strangers, people in anguish, and tell them that their dead son wanted them to know he was okay.

"I debated it for a week or so," June said later. "Who was I to call these people and tell them something like this? They're hurting enough." Who was that boy, anyway? She went through the previous days' newspapers and found a story about the accident, accompanied by a picture. His name was Andrew Miracolo. For days, June looked at his picture. This poor child, she thought. And these poor parents. She wanted to pass on his message, but a hundred questions swirled through her mind: If I do it, how will they react? Will they think I'm crazy? Or worse, cruel? How can I tell them? On the other hand, there was their son to consider—and the possibility that this might actually help. *Please, please tell my mom and dad I'm okay.* The problem wasn't June's own belief. She was convinced I had connected with that boy. The question was whether his parents would believe it.

June thought it would be easier if she didn't have to make a cold contact. She asked Tony and his wife, Ro, if they knew the family. They didn't, but Ro was a hairdresser who knew a lot of people through her work. Maybe one of her customers knew the family. Ro made a few calls, but came up empty. She did have an idea, though: send a sympathy card. That might soften the blow. That sounded right to June. Write to them. Much better than a phone call.

The Miracolos were unlisted in the phone book, so June went to the death notices in the newspaper. She found a listing for Andrew which included the name of the funeral director. She called the funeral home and said she wanted to send a sympathy card to the family.

Would they give her the Miracolos' address? She was told that the address couldn't be released, but that she could send the card to the funeral home and it would be forwarded.

There was one other piece of information that June learned from the death notice, and it startled her. It also strengthened her resolve to pass Andrew's message on to his parents. It said that Andrew's father was named Anthony. "I realized that the Tony that Andrew was talking about in the reading was his father, not my friend Tony," June said. When she saw that, she began to cry.

Still, two more days went by as June thought about what to say. Finally, she decided to ask for help from the person who started all this. "Andrew," she said, "if you really want me to do this, tell me what to say." She thinks he may have answered her, because that night, it all came to her, the words flowing much more easily than she imagined they would. On a sheet of lined looseleaf paper, she wrote:

Dear Mr. and Mrs. Miracolo,

My name is June Castonguay. I did not know Andrew or anyone in your family. I have friends that live in Bethpage. I happened to be there on the day of the accident. My friends' children were at the scene.

First, let me say I have been procrastinating about writing this letter. My fear was that you would think this was a cruel joke or that I was crazy. Neither is true. I myself am the mother of two children. I can't even imagine what you're going through. Please know before I begin that my prayers and my heart are with you.

On Friday was the terrible accident. On the following Tuesday I went to a psychic named John Edward. In his reading to me, he talked about this accident. He told me I had a big responsibility to see that this message got through to your family. He said the spirit wants his father and his family to know he is OK and happy and not to worry about him, and to prove it was him to say there was a birthday coming up in the family. The psychic wanted to know who Anthony was. I assumed it was my friend's son who was there.

But when I tried to get your address through the obituary in the paper, I saw Anthony was Andrew's dad.

I don't know if you believe in any of this or not. If you don't then please throw this in the garbage. If you feel comforted in any way that it might be true then I know it was worth the risk. Please, please know this in no way was meant to hurt anyone. But if I did not write this letter I would never know if I did the right thing or not. If for any reason you would like to talk to me or the psychic, here are our phone numbers . . .

June signed the letter, folded it neatly, and put it inside a condolence card. She sealed them in an envelope. "Then I kissed the letter up to God," she said, "hoping I was doing the right thing."

Mary Miracolo went to her mailbox and sorted through the sympathy cards that were still coming in. It was less than two weeks since the accident. When she came to one that was addressed to the family in care of the funeral home, Mary assumed it was from someone who had read about Andrew's death in the newspaper. She read the card, then opened the letter. The opening confused her, but then, midway through, she was thunderstruck. She began to scream, "I got my letter! I got my letter!"

She could hardly believe it. It seemed too good to be true, almost surreal. In her hysterics the day after Andrew died, she had wished he could write her a letter saying he was all right. She knew right away that this was it. Mary called June Castonguay to thank her, to find out if there was more, and the two women talked for more than an hour. June, in turn, learned that the birthday wish Andrew had expressed during the reading was for his father. Tony Miracolo's birthday was July 22, three days after the reading. It was a conversation June would never forget. She had worried how her letter would be received, whether she was doing the right thing. She could never have imagined how right it was.

I didn't talk to June after her reading, so I didn't find out until much later that she had delivered Andrew's message—and that it had actually come in response to his mother's desperate plea for comfort.

Nor did I know that in their phone conversation, June suggested to Mary that she come to see me. (The full story I relate here was pieced together after the fact.) And I certainly didn't know all the intriguing twists yet to come, including the fact that I had a previous connection to the Miracolos.

Though she was deeply affected and comforted by June's letter and what she said on the phone, Mary was in no shape to come to me for a reading at that point. "After we lost Andy, it was very bad here," she recalled. "Nobody could talk, nobody could stand up, nobody could eat. It was horrendous. Tony went in this corner, I went in that corner. It was like I lost my son, I lost my husband, I lost my other son.

"I told people about the letter. And they were telling me to go for a reading. They gave me books: *Life after Life* by Raymond Moody, books about mediums and spirit communication." Considering how Andrew had come through June, Mary thought he would be pleased if she and Tony came for their own reading. "But first I had to be able to stand up," Mary said. "I had to get my breath back. I needed to get some order in my life. I'm a teacher and a teacher has to have order."

Tony, meanwhile, needed much more than order. He needed time, and a lot of it. Andy's tragic death had sucked the life out of him. "He was in a living, breathing coma," Mary said, and an hour with a medium was not going to bring him out of it. It had nothing to do with any skepticism about the afterlife or about the spirit's ability to communicate from the Other Side. Tony had always believed the spirit lives on, and his conversion to Buddhism only strengthened this faith. What was more, only three years before, Tony himself had had a near-death experience that provided evidence that we do pass from one kind of existence to another when we die. Here is his description of the episode.

"It was in January of 1991. I collapsed in my bathroom one night, knocked out with a bleeding ulcer. I had thrown up blood earlier but I didn't get any medical help because I thought I had a stomach virus. And while I was unconscious I had an out-of-body experience. I was lying on the bathroom floor, and I later found out I was unconscious. Then I was above my body looking down. And I felt really good, really happy and light, and I was zipping around the bathroom. Then all of a sudden a hand hit me on my left shoulder and I heard a voice, a female voice. It said to me, 'You have to go back.' I never saw an angel or anything like that, I just felt a hand and heard the voice. And I remember communicating that I didn't want to go back because I was feeling so good. But then I was put back into my body, and as I was descending down to my body I did see a light, like a fiery glow, more yellow than white. It was above me. And then I began to wake up, and the first thing I felt was my right cheek against the cold ceramic floor. I found out later that I lost a third of my blood and did almost die."

Andrew, thirteen at the time, stayed with his father as they waited for help. Andrew was terrified. "Please, God, don't take my father," he cried. As fate would have it, God took Andrew three-and-a-half years later, leaving his father behind in deep despair, seemingly unable to go on. Some people respond to the death of someone close by coming to me immediately, hoping for some way to connect one last time. Others, especially parents who lose a child suddenly and without warning, need some time. The length varies. While Tony could not see how something like this would help, Mary was getting closer.

About six months after Andrew's death, the lights in his mother's car kept going on by themselves, and she believed that it was a sign from Andrew that he wanted to connect more directly with his family. When it happened again, she said, "Okay, Andrew, I'll call John Edward. I promise you." Her friend and neighbor, Anna, had been pushing her to do it, trying to soft-pedal any spookiness. "We'll just go in the daytime—what could happen?" Anna said.

Mary and Anna appeared at my door on February 11, 1995, seven months after Andrew passed. I, of course, had no idea who she was, but when I opened the door and saw her, I was struck by a great force. I pointed right at her and said, "Is there a Tony connected to you?"

The energy around Mary was so strong that I had a sudden and overpowering feeling that I should document the reading I was about to do. Now, this was weird. I had asked my part-time assistant, Ellen, to come by and take notes during the reading before this one, for a man named Keith. This was because I was contemplating leaving my job at the hospital to work as a medium full-time, and my guides had been telling me that a book like the one you are reading would be in my future. They told me that a session scheduled for that day would be literally one for the books, and that I should have a good record of it. I had never done this before, but I had found that ignoring my guides was never a good thing to do. They hadn't steered me wrong yet.

So the day before, I'd called Ellen and asked her to come over, thinking it was Keith's reading I was meant to document. Keith said it was all right with him, and Ellen took notes of the session on a yellow legal pad. I was puzzled when there wasn't anything special about the reading. But when Mary came next, and I asked her about "Tony" right at the front door, I realized I had been off by one reading. It was *her* session I was supposed to document. I asked Ellen, "Any way you can stay?" She had a lot to do that day, but as she told me later, something told her she wasn't going anywhere. We both thought at the time that it was my guides helping me with a book. We didn't know an entirely different force was at work.

Ellen sat down beside Mary and took out her pad and pen. I asked Mary if I could hold something of hers, and she gave me a bracelet. Mary had told me at the door that Tony was her husband, and I, assuming he was an anxious spirit, expected him to come through first. But the spirit world is nothing if not unpredictable. For reasons that will become clear, this is a case where I think it's important to present a transcript of the reading. It is edited only slightly, for brevity.

JOHN: *The first thing that's coming through is your son. Do you have a son who's passed?*

MARY: *Yes.*

JOHN: *Has he passed in the last two years? Did he pass in June or July?*

MARY: *Yes.*

JOHN: *Who's Tony? Is that his dad? Please let his father know he's okay. Very important. He says Dad's all alone, lost.*

MARY: *That's true.*

JOHN: *He's showing me a lacrosse stick.*

MARY: *His dad coaches lacrosse.*

JOHN: *Is his father a teacher? Because he's showing me my high school. I went to Glen Cove High.*

MARY: *He teaches at Glen Cove. You know him.*

JOHN: *I know his father? Don't say his name. Normally I wouldn't say Glen Cove High School, I'd just say high school. Hold on. Is this an impact passing? Is this a vehicular kind of thing? Was he hit by a car? Was he on a bicycle?*

MARY: *Yes, he was.*

JOHN: *He wants you to know he's okay. Who's Robert?*

MARY: *His grandpa.*

JOHN: *He wants him to know he's okay. And who's Mary, besides you? Has your husband's mother passed?*

MARY: *No.*

JOHN: *It's on his side of the family. Was the passing Andrew's fault?*

MARY: *I don't know. That's what we're trying to find out.*

JOHN: *Because in a very minor, minor way he's telling me the accident was his fault. He's showing me my bicycle when I was a kid. With a humongous flag. It's not that, right? I feel like he wasn't visible. Was this in a residential area?*

MARY: *(Nods).*

JOHN: *I feel like he jutted out. I feel like he's taking responsibility for this. She might have been going faster than she should have, but I feel like he was the one who jutted out. Is he Johnny? Or Joey? Who's that?*

MARY: *His friend.*

JOHN: *And Steven? Who's the "S"?*

MARY: *Steph?*

JOHN: *Is that his friend?*

MARY: *Yes. Girlfriend.*

JOHN: *Who's Danny?*

MARY: *Another friend.*

JOHN: *Was he in seventh grade, or sixth grade?*

MARY: *No.*

JOHN: *Was he sixteen or seventeen?*

MARY: *Sixteen.*

JOHN: *He was showing me a six or a seven. Feels like there's a distance between you and your husband. Instead of coming close together, you're here and he's there. You guys need to talk, to get connected again.*

MARY: *I know, but I don't know how to do that. His father is very much hurting.*

JOHN: *He says you have to tell his father he's okay. It's important. He needs to . . . I feel like there's a constant waterflow of emotions. He has not dealt with this and it's important that he knows that his son is okay. He has to give himself the time and opportunity. The grief seems like he just cuts it off. You're more accepting of this passing. It doesn't mean you like it any more. He just had so many aspirations and like, "He was a smart kid. Why did this happen?"*

MARY: *Does he have a message for his brother?*

JOHN: *He might not, so don't look for that. Does he have his shoes or his sneakers?*

MARY: *Andy was wearing his father's sneakers.*

JOHN: *Who's Chris—who's the "C" or "K"?*

MARY: *Friend.*

JOHN: *Does he have a ring? Or does your husband have his ring?*

MARY: *He has a watch.*

JOHN: *He's showing me something symmetrical. Did your husband want to give him one of his rings and he didn't get an opportunity to? He's talking about a ring. . . . Did he play hockey?*

MARY: *That's what I was looking for.*

JOHN: *And you buried him with a jersey?*

MARY: *Not with a jersey, but a hockey stick on his headstone.*

JOHN: *Because I see something sportswise. Did you have a floral thing made with sports?*

MARY: *Yes, the room was filled with floral arrangements in hockey motifs, and his hockey jersey was hanging.*

JOHN: *Also, does his father have something around his neck that was Andy's?*

MARY: *He wanted a chain but he didn't get it and when he died [Tony] went out and got it for himself.*

JOHN: *A gold chain?*

MARY: *Yes. Andy wanted one and he never got it. And out of the clear blue my husband went out and bought the same chain Andy wanted, without knowing which one it was. And my husband never liked chains or jewelry.*

JOHN: *Okay, tell your husband he was guided to buy that by his son. I must not have had him [as a teacher]. Because I keep asking him to tell me who the teacher is.*

MARY: *I'm sure you had him. Because when I walked in I knew you knew him.*

JOHN: *You did?*

MARY: *It was the way you said his name.*

JOHN: *Now I want to know who it is! I'll go room to room [in the high school building] . . . Okay, I just said, "Take me into the building," and he took me in the front entrance. And I said, "Should I go right?" And he said no. So I said, "Should I go straight?" And he said yes. So I went straight and he gave me the feeling it's downstairs on the first hallway. Yes?*

MARY: *Yes.*

JOHN: *Don't tell me. I will get it. I know who it is . . . does he teach social studies?*

MARY: *(Nods).*

JOHN: *You know how I know? Because your son said to me . . . I said, "Do something that I would understand, that I would identify with one of my teachers." The only teacher who ever threw me out of a class . . . Mr. Miracolo?*

MARY: *(Nods and smiles).*

JOHN: *I knew it! He was the only teacher to ever throw me out of a class. I had a trigonometry class that I wasn't ready for the next period. And I asked your husband for a pass to go to the bathroom. And instead I went to an extra help class for trig. And when I came back, Mr. Miracolo looked at me and said, "You—out!" And your son showed me that. He wants you to know he's okay. Did he have a certain restaurant he used to go all the time? They have a mirror up in this restau-*

rant with like scratchy glass on it, like you can kind of see through it but you can't. I feel almost like your husband was looking in that mirror and he saw your son. Your son's confirming that you did see him when you thought you saw him.

MARY: *Does he know how much we love him?*

JOHN: *Just understand that this whole session comes through to you out of love.*

At this point, Mary told me the story of how she came to me: how she'd prayed for a letter from Andrew and how the letter came through June Castonguay. She also said there was, in fact, a time at a restaurant when she thought she saw Andrew's image in a mirror. This was a great comfort to her because there were several instances when Mary thought she saw images of Andrew in photographs, though Tony was skeptical. (In addition, in pictures taken at Andrew's wake, a pink glow seemed to hover around the coffin.)

Mary thought the most poignant thing that came through during the reading was Andy's reference to the gold chain his father was wearing around his neck. She explained that a few months before the accident, Andy and she had gone to a flea market, where he practically begged her for a gold chain he saw in a jeweler's booth. She said no—it was too expensive—and Andy had a fit. A few months after Andy was killed, Tony, though in his deep depression, announced that he wanted a gold chain. He was aware that Andy had wanted a chain, but still this struck Mary as very strange, even as a tribute. Tony disliked jewelry generally, and always made fun of men—particularly men who were, like him, of Italian descent—who wore gold chains. He thought it was tacky. But he and Mary went to the flea market and she took him to the jewelry booth. And to Mary's amazement, Tony picked out the very same chain Andy had wanted, without knowing which one it was.

Mary had no trouble believing me when I said that Andy had guided his father to do this. "He wants you to know you're as close to him as the chain around his father's neck," I told Mary. But what neither of us knew was that at this very moment, as she was sitting with me, Tony was back at the flea market. On the spur of the moment, and without telling Mary, Tony had decided to get a gold "20" to put on the chain. That was Andy's number on the high school hockey team.

But Andy wasn't finished yet. His mother still needed him.

Three months later, just after Memorial Day, Sandra and I got married and flew to Bora Bora, an island in the South Pacific near Tahiti, for our honeymoon. It was an idyllic place, and I was in love and on vacation. But late in the morning a day after we arrived, I was sunning myself on the oceanfront deck outside our hut when I felt a warm sensation on the back of my neck. It wasn't Sandra. It was the feeling I usually get when I'm tuned out and a spirit wants to get my attention. We were not alone.

Damn, I thought. *Leave me alone. I'm on my honeymoon. I'm off duty.* But spirits are not always respectful. In this case, to make matters just a little bit more annoying, the spirit was giving me messages in French, a language I don't understand. I kept hearing the words *avec moi,* over and over. I asked Sandra what they meant and she told me, "With me." I assumed that since we were on a French-speaking island, it was, shall we say, a local spirit.

But then, with those words I was shown Mary Miracolo's face. I was seeing her, and also getting a feeling of her—a strong combination that definitely made me sit up and take notice. Instantly, I knew that it was Andrew who was coming through. And he was coming through with severely negative emotional feelings, such deep, intense despair that I was soon on the verge of tears myself. I knew that Andrew was making me feel the anguish that someone in his family was feeling. I wasn't sure if it was his mother, but someone in that family was at the end of their rope, and might be on the verge of something terrible. I didn't want to bring work into our honeymoon so I told Sandra I didn't feel so good and needed to take a walk.

We were in a row of huts connected by planks at the oceanfront, and I started walking along the boards, trying to shake this awful feeling. But I couldn't. Andrew wasn't letting me go. Then, with a powerful feeling of urgency, he was telling me I had to get some kind of tape to his family. I came back to the hut and told Sandra what was going on. I reminded her of the teenager killed on his bicycle whose mother had come to me in a roundabout way a few months before and whose father had once thrown me out of social studies class. "This kid Andrew is coming through about a tape," I said. "I don't know what he means, but he's giving me just a terrible, terrible feeling."

I remembered Mary Miracolo was the one whose reading I had asked Ellen to sit in on and take notes. Sandra wondered if she had taped the reading. No, I said. She took notes on a legal pad. Ellen knew better than anyone that while I encourage clients to take notes during readings, I don't like to be taped because it makes me self-conscious. Andrew's mother had brought a tape recorder herself, and I'd asked her to take notes instead.

Better call Ellen anyway, Sandra thought. She might have an idea what this is about. "If something bad happens and you don't do anything about it, I don't want to have to live with you," Sandra added.

I called New York. Ellen was shocked to hear my voice. "Where are you?" she asked through a faint connection.

"I'm in Bora Bora," I said.

"What are you doing, calling all the way from there?"

"Do you remember Andrew?"

"Mary's Andrew?"

"Yeah. He's here. He's pounding me over the head. He's talking about a tape. Ellen, did you tape that reading?"

There was a pause.

"Ellen?"

"Um, I did." She admitted she'd used the recorder she always kept in her briefcase. She started blurting out excuses, "You talk too fast; you made it sound so important, I didn't want to rely on my notes if you ever wanted a transcript"—but I wasn't mad at her. I was just glad to solve the mystery, and to satisfy Andrew's wishes and his mother's need.

"Listen," I said, "call that kid's mother and get her that tape. I don't know why, but her son wants her to have that tape." Actually, though Andrew had first given me the image and feeling of his mother, I thought that was just so I would know who was coming through. Using my logical mind, rather than my psychic one, I suspected it was his father who needed the tape. I remembered how he was having a harder time dealing with the loss, and I guessed that Mary wanted the tape to show him that Andrew had really come through at the reading.

Ellen called Mary and heard yet another amazing story about the ability of spirits to show us that they haven't left us, that they are still connected to us in sometimes elusive but profound ways. It seems that at virtually the same time that Andrew came through to me, late in the morning in the South Pacific, it was late at night in New York and his mother was having a crisis of faith. She was reaching out to Andrew for help once more.

"Though I'd had this wonderful reading in February, things were still very bad at home," Mary explains. "Tony had been impressed when I told him about the reading, but he still was not talking. Around Memorial Day, Tony's brother came up from Florida and he and Tony and Matthew went out one night. I was alone, and I just cried my eyes out. I couldn't take any more silence. I was going to church, I was praying, we went to bereavement groups, but we still couldn't sit down to dinner together. And it all came out that night. I said, 'Andy, if God can let you do one more favor, give me a sign, just to tell me it's going to get better. I can deal with it if I know it's going to get better than this. Just give me anything to let me know it's going to be all right.' Nobody knew I cried myself to sleep that night except God and Andy."

The morning after that horrible night, Mary went out for a walk. When she came back there was a message on her answering machine. It was Ellen, asking her to call her as soon as she got in. "I knew right away that somehow Andy got through," Mary says. She called

Ellen, who told her about my call from Bora Bora. "John says Andrew told him he needs to get this tape to his father." Mary didn't react, not until Ellen dropped off the tape later that day. "It's not for Tony," Mary said. "It's for me."

"When that tape came into my home, healing began," Mary says. "We turned the corner. Not because we listened to the tape. I didn't need to hear it. Because I was firmly convinced that Andy heard me and he never left me. He only left me physically. And he's much more alive, in a sense, because he can do *anything*. He brought us together. He tried to heal us."

Those last thoughts of Mary's are what I focus on when I consider this episode: her astute and spiritually aware observation that we do rise up when we die, to a power we on this side can only imagine. We move on to a much higher form of existence—a graduation of sorts. In that sense, while the process of dying can be painful, and while the aftermath can be emotionally excruciating for those left behind, we can at least take comfort from the fact that the departed are—as clichéd as it sounds—in a better place, and yet still connected to us. That's what comes through all the time: they're all right, don't worry. And they're still with us.

Can they do *anything* on the Other Side? I don't know about that. I believe that some souls can do more than others, depending on where they are in their journeys. What I do know is that Andrew's soul is evolved enough that he is able to do things I find amazing. He is among the most powerful, loving, and determined spirits I have encountered.

Take, for instance, everything that had to occur for his mother to get the comfort she needed. First, Andrew had to come through to June, a stranger. He had to come through forcefully enough to convince her that she was doing the right thing by writing to his family. June feels he even helped her write the letter. Then, the tape. Why was Ellen there the day of Mary's reading? Where did I get the feeling that I needed to document the reading, and why did I end up with not just a pad of notes but a cassette tape? Yes, the tape has helped me relate this story with accuracy. (It yielded the transcript on the previous pages.) But now I know that it was not so much for me as for Mary, who now keeps the tape in a jewelry box. And as Mary says, it wasn't about what was on the tape. If it was, my guides, or Andy's spirit, would have told me to allow Mary herself to tape the session. But I said no, leading Ellen to do it. That turned out to be the thing that validated that Andrew was listening and answering his mother's prayers. Obviously, her own tape would not have had that effect.

There are other things that have led me to marvel at Andrew's powers, some of which came up in later encounters with his family. In March 1996, a year after her reading, Mary brought her surviving son, Matthew, to me, and true to form, Andy's spirit came through vividly again. "Your brother's being very cute," I told him at one point. "He's got another name, a nickname. It sounds maybe Russian or Polish." All his friends called him Androskiday, Matthew told me. Andy also reminded me that day he had a girlfriend when he passed: Her birthday was today, and now she was dating one of his best friends. "He wants you to say Happy Birthday for him," I said. Mary confirmed that Andy's girlfriend, Stephanie, was in fact now dating his friend Michael, but neither she nor Matthew knew whether it was her birthday. When she got home, Mary called Michael and asked him. "Yeah, how'd you know?" he said.

Nine months later, Tony Miracolo decided he was ready to connect with Andy. "When I'm driving home, I feel his presence, almost like he's holding my leg," Tony told Mary. "I feel him and I cry. I can't shake it." Mary said she would make a reading with me her Christmas present to him. It was December 1996, two-and-a-half years after Andy passed. Tony says he wasn't looking for confirmation; he believed there was strong contact between Andy and the family. But he felt a desire to have a more direct firsthand experience.

In this visit, Andy told me that his father had built a shrine in dedication to him. "It's a religious shrine but it's not Catholic," I said. "It's in the right corner of your yard and you built it right after your son died." Tony confirmed that he had built a Buddhist shrine in Andy's honor, and that it was on the right side of the yard. "And

Andy wants you to know," I said, "that when you were building it, every stone you laid he held your hand."

Andy also began telling me about a trip his family had recently taken. He showed me deep blue water. "You and your wife went walking one day," I told Tony. "She went this way, you went that way. You took a picture of a stone wall or a castle or something made of stone."

"That's right," Tony said.

"Well, your son stepped in front of the camera when you took the picture."

Mary said she knew exactly what I was talking about. She had a photograph from that trip—a cruise to Greece—showing a stone castle. And in the middle of the photo was a bright light. She didn't need me to tell her what it was. "As soon as it was developed I knew it was him," Mary said.

She also reports that Andy actually called out on that trip. "We were in the cabin on the cruise ship, I woke up and heard, '*Maaaa*.' Tony said the next day to Matthew, 'Why did you wake us up?' Matthew said, 'I didn't do that.' It's not a coincidence that it was so peace-filled, that vacation."

Calling out like that takes an incredible amount of energy on the part of a spirit, another indication of Andrew's power. Why was Andy's voice so strong from the Other Side? For one thing, there is the strength of his mother and father's own spirituality and faith in a life beyond this one. Their ability to receive his messages is part of the picture. There is also evidence that Andy had always been very spiritually connected himself, in ways that even he wasn't aware of. His parents explain that they realized this after I told them during one reading that Tony's grandfather, who passed before Andy was born, was his spirit guide.

"My son always had an imaginary friend named Jimmy," Tony said. "And he would walk around talking to 'Jimmy,' just constantly babbling to him all the time. Andy was a stutterer, and once Mary's father heard Andy talking to 'Jimmy' in the basement and he wasn't stuttering. But when he came back upstairs, he was stuttering again.

He was still talking to Jimmy when he got older, and we began to worry about it. He was sixteen and still doing it, pretending he was a sportscaster, with Jimmy as his sidekick. And in all the years, I never connected it. My grandfather's name was Vincent, but everyone called him Jimmy." It clicked for Mary and Tony when I told them Andy wanted them to know that his great-grandfather was his spirit guide. And it made them realize that he had probably lived his entire life connected to the spirit world in a way that would enable him to reconnect strongly with this side when he passed. And they mentioned something else that clicked for me: Andrew's last name, Miracolo, means "miracle" in Italian.

I will leave you with one last story about Andrew, and I consider it a kind of legacy. On our honeymoon, Sandra and I spent a day in Los Angeles before flying to the islands, and saw the movie *Casper*. I liked the music and bought the soundtrack when we got home a couple of weeks later. I unwrapped the CD and popped it into the player in my car. I was driving on the North Shore of Long Island on a beautiful June day, just two weeks removed from the morning Andrew came through to me as I sunbathed at the edge of the South Pacific. A song finished, but before the next one began, I heard, between the tracks, a voice clearly say: "For my mom and dad and from your mother."

It was the "from your mother" part that stunned me. As comfortable as I am with the spirit world, connections to my mother always unnerve me. Confused and distracted, I almost ran into a pickup truck stopped at a light in front of me. I slammed on my brakes, stopping just a foot away from the pickup. And my eyes went right to one spot on its bumper. It said, "Andrew." It was on an "I survived Hurricane Andrew" bumper sticker.

I pulled over to compose myself and take all this in. Then, instantly, I got a feeling that the next song, the one for Andrew's parents and from my mother, would be about the love that continues between this side and the Other Side. The song came on. It was *Remember Me This Way*, sung by Jordan Hill, and as it played I felt I was being told that this was a kind of psalm to the spirit world. They told me to listen to the song as though the source and recipient of the verses was meant to alternate between the physical world and the spirit world. In other words, some verses were meant as messages from us to them, others from them to us.

I sat at the roadside, knowing that the connections with Andrew now involved my mother's love for me. I listened to the song, and absorbed the feeling I got with each verse. When it was a verse meant as a sentiment from us to them, I got a feeling of sending out and up. When it was from them to us, I had the feeling of a presence behind my shoulders. I listened closely as the traffic whizzed by, loving the music, knowing that it said everything that needed to be said about love between worlds—knowing that the love lasts forever and our loved ones are forever in our hearts.

THEY'RE IN CHARGE (PART 2)

I have become fairly adept at opening and closing myself to spirit communication. I say "fairly" because it doesn't always work quite as well as a simple switch. I can open myself to spirit vibrations so that messages come through more vigorously and clearly. And I can close myself off so that I don't walk through life constantly bombarded by messages. But—as the story of Andrew shows—there are times when there's no holding them back. If they want to come through, they're going to come through.

I have walked through shopping malls and picked up messages. I have been at parties and other large gatherings where I know a spirit is trying to come through. But as much as I hate to thwart a spirit, it takes an extraordinary one to get me to approach a stranger and start delivering a message from the Other Side. That has happened (as in the case of the spirit who got me to call her mother during a reading) but thankfully not often.

14

As Andrew reminded me, I'm never really off duty, even on my honeymoon. And he wasn't the only spirit who showed up that week and made something happen (signaling to Sandra that she wasn't just marrying into a family, she was marrying into a crowd) and they had a habit of showing up unannounced day or night.

On our way home from Bora Bora, we landed in Los Angeles, planning to stay one night before flying home the next morning. I told the cab driver at the L.A. airport the name of our hotel, but he couldn't find it, and after forty-five minutes of driving around, I told him to stop. We were in front of a very expensive-looking hotel called the Bel Age. I went in, gave the desk clerk the name of the hotel, and asked if he knew where it was. Hearing this, another man behind the counter said, "You don't want to stay there."

"I don't?" I asked.

"No. You want to stay here. This is much nicer."

"I'm sure it is," I said, "but we have reservations at this other hotel. We just want to get there and check in. We're pretty tired."

The man was the manager. "Come with me," he said, and brought me up to a huge, beautiful room. He said he would charge us just $75. There was definitely something odd about this—it had to be a $200-a-night room. I strongly suspected this was being orchestrated by a spirit. I just didn't know who or why. I figured maybe it was just a perk, a spiritual thank-you for helping out Andrew and his mother while on my honeymoon. I called Sandra in, and we went upstairs to our room. A few minutes later, the phone rang. It was the manager again. He had made dinner reservations for us across the street, at the very trendy restaurant Spago. Yes, a big thank-you. We hadn't planned on such an upscale night.

Soon after we sat down at our table, I began getting flashes of information about one of the waiters. Every time he walked by, I would hear something: his name, where he lived, other personal information. I told Sandra, who, having downed two glasses of white zinfandel, decided to have some fun with it. The next time the waiter walked by, she said, "Are you Phillip?"

"Yes," he said with a smile. Sandra told him she was "a well-known New York psychic" and gave him the information I had gotten. "C'mon," he said. "Are you with the FBI? How do you know this stuff?"

"No, I told you I'm a psychic," she said playfully. Each time he walked by she would give him something else I had gotten, and he would say, "C.I.A.?"

Then I got the name Michael, and when Phillip passed, she said, "Is there a Michael around you?"

With that, Phillip stopped in his tracks and his attitude changed completely. We had obviously hit a nerve. He became emotional and said, "How do you know that?" It got too serious too quickly for Sandra, and she stammered, "I . . . I . . . ." She pointed to me. "He's really the psychic, not me. Talk to him." My mouth full of pasta, I nodded. Phillip sat down with us. "Tell me about Michael," he said softly. I briefly explained what I do and began doing an impromptu reading. I told him that Michael was coming through and telling me that he, Phillip, was about to fly to New York for some kind of memorial, and that he was thanking Phillip for coming. Michael also wanted Phillip to tell his mother and his sister that he was all right.

Michael and Phillip were lovers. Michael had died of AIDS a year before. And yes, Phillip said, he was leaving the next day for a one-year-later memorial. When Michael stepped back, Phillip said, "I can't thank you enough. You've given me such peace." He got up and told the headwaiter that he had to go home.

I realized that all this *was* orchestrated by the Other Side. To get this message to Phillip, Michael had to put us in a cab whose driver wouldn't find our hotel, so we would get to the other hotel, where the manager would make us an offer we couldn't refuse, so he could send us across the street to meet Phillip, the Spago waiter. Thus, Sandra began her life married to a medium.

As you're probably guessing by now, Sandra is a very open-minded person who generally rolls with the punches. But being married to a psychic has not always been easy for her, especially when my spirit guides come through with important information that I use to advise her. For instance, if there's a decision to make, they will often give me a positive or negative feeling that guides me down the right path. They have never steered me wrong, and I have come to value and depend on them. But because I'm constantly seeing things and expressing them to Sandra, I've sometimes been guilty of lecturing, almost acting like an overbearing father—do this, don't do that—based on what my guides are saying to me. To be sure, Sandra has her life and needs to be able to make her own decisions based on what she wants, not on what *they* are telling me. On the other hand, I wonder, "Well, why wouldn't she want this information?" Clearly, a balance has to be struck, and that's something I struggle with: When do I say it, when do I not? In a reading, I say everything, but what is the ethic in my personal life—not only with my wife, but with friends and relatives? Maybe that's one of the lessons I have to learn.

In the end, we both know there's no controlling spirits. One night Sandra came home and as she tried to open the front door of our house, it felt as though someone was holding it closed. She thought it was me, playing games. But when she finally got it open, she saw that I wasn't home yet. That whole evening, until I got home, she had that "being watched" feeling. Our dog, who loves to jump around and play, just hopped on Sandra's lap and stayed there. Then, while e-mailing a friend upstairs, she heard a "ruffling" noise. She finally decided one of "John's people" was in the house. "All right, whoever you are," she announced, "John's not here. Come back tomorrow." When I got home and she told me what had happened, I felt an energy too, but by now it wasn't strong. We later realized what was going on. Earlier that evening, before she got home and I went out, a couple had shown up for a reading—a day early. They had written the wrong date on their calendar. When they came back for their appointment the next day, I recognized the first spirit that came through as the one that had been there the night before.

I have had many other experiences in which spirits have come at unexpected times, and in unexpected ways, making me feel like a messenger carrying a package with a name but no address. Finding the recipient became part of the job.

I was sitting on the beach one summer day when I felt the spirit of a young male trying to come through. He gave me the name Jason. I have a cousin whose son's name is Jason, and my first thought was that something happened to him. I immediately called her to make sure everything was okay. She assured me Jason was fine, and I went back to the beach. But Jason came with me. Now, he was saying, "orange slices." I sat there trying to figure this out. *Orange slices? What is this?*

Information began pouring through. Whoever this Jason was, he told me he wanted his mother to know he was fine, that he was with her, and that the path she was on was the right one. He told me that his mother wanted a message and that she trusted me to receive and deliver one. I grabbed a notebook and started writing down everything he was showing me. These things have a way of explaining themselves later on.

Jason showed me a teddy bear, a cap and gown, and an out-of-state wedding that took place after he passed. He showed me that he had died recently and accidentally, but that his actions had led to his passing; that he had impact to his head and chest. He said he was with his grandfather, whose name had an "R" sound, along with a young male to his side, an "M" name who had cancer. He said he was one of three boys. A birthday was coming soon. He made a big deal about a new dog.

I thought about this for the next two days. Especially the orange slices. It seemed so specific. Finally, on Tuesday, out of nowhere, it clicked. *Orange slices!* I had recently struck up an e-mail correspondence with a woman in Wyoming named Sandy. We had been introduced on-line by Judy Guggenheim, author of *Hello from Heaven!*, and had exchanged a few e-mails about an upcoming conference in Philadelphia she was helping organize, and which I had agreed to attend. And in one of our e-mail conversations, we had somehow gotten on the subject of those candied citrus fruits that come in slices, covered in sugar. We both liked the orange ones best, and Sandy had promised to bring some to Philadelphia when we met. Orange slices! And yes—Jason! I was pretty sure she had told me her son's name was Jason.

Early the next morning, I got Sandy's phone number from Judy and called her. This is John Edward, I blurted. Sandy later told me I was talking so fast she didn't catch my name at first and thought I was a salesman. When she realized who I was, I asked her what she was doing Monday afternoon, around 3:30. Did she have a "conversation" with her son? Did she ask him to give me a message?

Sandy said she couldn't remember exactly where she was at 3:30 on Monday. Doesn't matter, I said, and started reading to her from the notes I had taken. Sandy was overjoyed. Just about everything I said made sense to her. The cap and gown: Jason had graduated two months before he passed. The wedding: Sandy and her husband had gone to the out-of-state wedding of Jason's cousin. Jason's grandfather with the "R" name: Roy. His cousin with the "M" name and cancer: Matt, who died in a car accident but had cancer. He was one of three boys and the birthday coming up was that of one of his brothers, in two weeks (and his father's in three). The new dog. The characteristics of his death—all true.

But what made the most sense of all to Sandy was the big message. "He said that he knew you wanted a message and that you trusted me," I told her. "He says he didn't drop the ball." When I finished, Sandy told me that she had asked for just this. "Since Jason left last summer," she said, "I've had conversations with him. I've said many times, 'If you can't get through directly to me, go through someone else.' I gave him the names of friends who I think might be receptive, and also mediums who I know are genuine. I gave him your name." She said she had felt a little silly doing this, "but you never know." And now she did know. Jason did not "drop the ball."

That day, Sandy sent another e-mail, this time posting it on an after-death communication message board. "He did just what I wanted, what I needed," she wrote of Jason. "He gave me the message in a way that I can't argue. I will not be able to 'let it go,' as I have been told in the past, but I will be able to 'let it be.' My son obviously has control and ability. I am flying high and shouting from the rooftops. I have certainty."

WINDS BENEATH OUR WINGS

Anthony Vanaria will never forget this moment. He was at the front door of his parents' home, about to leave, when his mother stopped him and said she had just seen the strangest thing. Anthony's father had been lying on the living room floor, watching television in his favorite spot, when she saw a brilliant glow around his body, and then a light "shoot out of him to the ceiling." She chuckled nervously as she described what she had seen.

Anthony, an instructor in emergency medical procedures for the New York City Fire Department who was then in his early twenties, came back in and looked at his father. He realized immediately something was very wrong. Kneeling down, he saw that his father had just suffered a massive heart attack. Anthony performed CPR, but he knew it was too late. His father was just a few months shy of his fiftieth birthday. For years afterward, Anthony felt guilty that his father had died while he was there—that he was an emergency medical worker who trained others, and still he could not save his own father. He would also never forget the apparition his mother saw as her husband was passing over. It would turn out to be only the beginning.

That night, Anthony recounts, he had the first of several dreams so vivid he would swear they were real. His description leads me to believe that in fact they were not dreams but visits from the Other Side. "The night my father died, he came to me," Anthony says. "He led me downstairs. He came through a door in the dining room, but it was a door that didn't actually exist. He was sitting there playing cards with his brother, who passed about a year before he did. I asked him how he was, and he said he was fine. I asked what it was like over there, and he said, 'It's really nice. You'll find out some day.' I asked him again, 'Well, what's it like?' And he said, 'I can't tell you.' Then he and his brother went through that door and I couldn't. And then I woke up."

A skeptic might say it was just a dream, triggered by the trauma of the death of Anthony's father that day. But since I know exactly what Anthony is talking about (many people have told me of similar experiences, and I've had several myself) I believe the evidence is that it was indeed a visit. Especially when considered against two more that came later, they are not so easily dismissed.

Shortly after Anthony's father died, his mother wanted to collect on his life insurance but she couldn't find the policy. At this point, Anthony's father came through to him again in a dream. He told his son where the insurance policy was. He had placed it with other important papers in a strongbox hidden in the attic. In the morning, he called his mother and told her where to look. It was just where his father said it would be.

Sometime after that, Anthony had a third visit. This time, it happened in a dream in which his three-year-old nephew, Marty, was trying to ride a bicycle. In the dream, the little boy's mother, Anthony's sister, turned to their father and said, "He's too young to ride a bike. He's only three." Their father replied, "It's all right. I'll teach him." Then he held on to the back of the bicycle as his grandson rode up and down the driveway. A few days later, Anthony heard from his sister that her son was riding a bicycle up and down the driveway. She couldn't get over it. After all, Marty was only three.

Six years later, Anthony's mother had a heart attack while driving. Her car crashed, and she was revived by paramedics, but remained in a vegetative state for several months. Anthony wanted to abide by what he knew were his mother's wishes, and let her go. But the hospital refused to disconnect her from life support. Finally, he prevailed and his mother was allowed to die. While he knew it was the right thing to do, it gave him only more pain. "I walked around with the worst grief I could ever imagine," Anthony later recalled. "I felt like I couldn't save my father's life and that I had just killed my mom."

A year or so after his mother passed, Anthony came to me for a reading. He had become interested in spirit communication after his father's death, and toyed with the idea of having a reading with a medium. The feeling had become stronger in the aftermath of his mother's passing. His decision to end life support had not been a popular one with everyone in the family, and Anthony couldn't shake his feelings of guilt, his worry that he had done the wrong thing. He hoped his mother would come through during a reading with a medium, and tell him he had done the right thing.

The moment finally came one summer evening when he and his wife found themselves walking up to my door as the sun was going down. As they waited for me to answer the doorbell, Anthony saw something that gave him a good feeling about the reading. Ever since his mother's death, he had kept seeing her birthday, February 22, in numerals: 222. Now, as he stood at my door, he noticed a car pull out of my driveway. Its license tag contained the numbers 222. He pointed it out to his wife and they looked at each other, as if to say: "They're waiting for us."

Anthony says that when he came inside my house, he had an "overjoyed" feeling. "It's hard to explain but I felt like I was attending a reunion."

During the reading, both Anthony's mother and father came

through. His father gave me his name and told me that he had passed of a heart attack. He asked me to send his love to Anthony. His mother, meanwhile, told me when she passed and said she wanted her son to stop feeling guilty. "She says she knows you did all you could for her. Her brain was gone and she thanks you for what you did. It was the right thing." Anthony started to cry. "I'm so relieved," he said. "Your father is asking about your son, Anthony the third," I said. "Well, he's not born yet," Anthony replied. "He's due in September. We know he's a boy and it's true, we've already decided to name him Anthony the third."

His father told me that a chain Anthony was wearing had been his. "That's true," Anthony said. "Your dad and mom are asking about a tattoo. Did you have a tattoo done in your dad's honor?" I asked. Anthony was wearing a warmup jacket. He took it off and rolled up his shirtsleeve to reveal the very top of his arm. It was a tattoo depicting a cross, bathed in light, and the words, "In Memory of Dad."

"Your mom says it's good for both of them," I told Anthony. He smiled. "I did feel weird just having one for him."

Toward the end of the reading, Anthony asked if he could pose a question to his father. Usually, if the energy is still strong I will facilitate that, but in this case I could feel they were pulling back. I told Anthony I couldn't maintain the contact, and he never got to ask his question. But as you will see, he did get his answer.

Anthony and his wife were married in 1995, and at the wedding, when he and his mother took the floor for the traditional mother-son dance, they expected to hear the song she had selected, "Mr. Wonderful." But instead the disc jockey put on "Wind Beneath My Wings," by Bette Midler—his parents' favorite song. Anthony found it upsetting to hear, and went to the DJ afterward to ask why he had switched the song. "I was told you requested it," the DJ said. By who? Anthony asked. "A man came up to me and said that's the song you wanted," the DJ said. Anthony asked him to point out the man; he was so upset, in fact, that he walked the DJ around the room, looking for the man. But he couldn't find him. He asked the DJ to describe him. "He described my dad exactly," Anthony says.

During our reading, Anthony's father had acknowledged his wedding, and said that he had been there. But that's all he said. The question Anthony wanted to ask was whether he had been the one who had told the DJ to play "Wind Beneath My Wings." For him it was a loose end of the reading.

When he and his wife got into their car to go home after the reading, Anthony says, "We had this strange feeling that I can't describe. That we were with my parents. I truly felt like I could feel them behind me. I started to drive away. I turned on the radio, and 'Wind Beneath My Wings' came on. My wife started to cry. I just pulled the car over. I looked up in the sky and thanked God and my parents for the beautiful gift they gave me."

P A R T   I I I

D E E P E R

Like anyone else, the thing I have wondered about most is what it's like on the Other Side. The truthful answer is: I don't know. And I am highly skeptical of any human being who says he does. No one can know until they get there.

But I do know what I think it *may* be like because I have had glimpses. There have been times when spirits have come through so clearly and strongly that I have said to them, "Tell me what it's like there. Give me an idea." This has been during readings, and my clients have no idea I'm doing it. Every time I have done this, I've gotten back the same feelings from the Other Side: *Just pass them the messages and don't worry about what it's like here. You'll find out when you get here.* The feeling they give me is that I'm like an annoyingly curious kid impatient to know things I wouldn't understand, and they're trying to get me to go away.

I feel as though we're on a need-to-know basis. They want us to know just enough about the Other Side—that it exists and that it's a positive place. They don't want us to become more worried about the Other Side than about the lives we're leading now. We all have jobs to do, lessons to learn.

I have managed to get them to give me a peek, consistent with much of what has been written about the nature of our spiritual existence. Once, I was given the image of a ladder, indicating that the Other Side is about our souls climbing to higher levels. Another time it was shown to me as a college campus: a series of large buildings with colossal columns, the largest one referred to as the "Hall of Knowledge." I don't think this was meant literally, but as a symbol of an existence in which we are required to graduate from one level to the next. But again, this is just a peek. It's like landing in India and never getting past the airport. You might get a slight sense of the place. You might see that they speak a different language and have different customs. But you're not getting inside. And until you do, you don't know what it's really like. But it does confirm, for me, the long-held belief that our current, physical life is only a brief stop on our soul's journey to higher levels of Godliness. How do we know these glimpses are indicative of the truth? Because people all over the world, through many centuries, have reported the same things. Near-death experiences have revealed the same "light" and beauty that draws us to the Other Side, and religions are based on the concept that we are constantly striving to reach higher levels of spirituality.

One presumption many people have is that the instant we cross over we immediately acquire ultimate wisdom. But spirits don't have all the answers. What I've inferred from some spirits I have encountered during readings is that they evolve at different paces, and what they know depends on whether they learned the lessons they were supposed to learn and where they are in their soul's progression. Some souls take longer than others to evolve.

Some spirits have told me that their work on the Other Side involves helping people over here. The spirit of one child told me he was helping other children cross over. In another reading, a spirit came through saying he had not completed his life lessons when he was in the physical body, and so his soul was not able to graduate to a higher level when it arrived on the Other Side. He had died young, at twenty-three, in an auto accident, and he had decided to complete his lessons by helping his teenage nephew, who was a lot like him. The reading was with this spirit's brother—the father of the boy he was now helping. When I passed this information on, the father cried. "Yes, he's just like my brother," he said. "He makes the same mistakes."

Perhaps the closest I have come to encountering the actual voices of the spirit side came several years ago, on a morning not long after I graduated from college. I had just stepped out of the shower and was lying on my bed. I didn't go to sleep; I was just in a mood to lay down and relax and think about the day ahead. And the next thing I knew, I was being taken to a place that had an infinite feeling to it. A place where, if you said something, it would echo on and on and on. It reminded me of the early scene in the movie *Superman*, on the planet Krypton. I felt as though I was standing in this vast, dark place with no beginning or end. And then I saw faces, the faces of many old men. At this point, I saw the words, "Counsel of Elders," just the way I saw words when I was a child. And then I heard those same words, just as I hear them, clairaudiently, during my readings. *Counsel of Elders.*

This doesn't necessarily mean that there is really such a thing as a "Counsel of Elders." More likely, this was their way of expressing the hierarchy of the spirit world in words I could understand. I also knew that my guides were part of this "counsel," though I couldn't tell which ones they were. This might help explain my abilities. It may not explain *why* I have them, but it does seem to make sense that someone whose spirit guides are at the higher levels of the spiritual realm would have a more direct connection to the Other Side.

The most vivid glimpse I've gotten of *what it's like over there* came as my aunt Rachel was dying of cancer in 1996. It came in a dream. And bear in mind that dreams are where we have our closest encounters with the Other Side because it's in this unconscious state that our own spirit, or *astral*, bodies are able to travel to the other realm and meet with spirits. As I've said earlier, this doesn't happen very often, but when it does, you know it: the details are incredibly vivid and unforgettable. I call these "lucid dreams," or "visits," and this was such a case for me.

My mother is knocking on my bedroom door, and I jump up. I look over at Sandra and she's sleeping. I look over at my dog, Jolie, and think, "Why isn't she barking?" Jolie yelps her head off if there's a squirrel outside, let alone a knock on the door. The bedroom door opens and my mother is standing there. She's in silhouette, bathed in the glow of the hallway light behind her. I can just make out her features. If this was happening in the conscious state, I would be running up to her, enveloping her in my arms. But in this state, I am just taking it in, almost unemotionally. She says, "Johnny, come . . . come with me." I say, "uh-uh"—I don't want to go. I think it means this is it for me. She looks at me, almost annoyed, and says, "Johnny, I want to show you something." I get up out of the bed and the sheets come off and . . . I'm on the Grand Central Parkway, not driving, exactly, but floating.

My mother points up at an apartment building called the Monte Excelsior—which is the name of an actual building near the parkway. She points up at the word "Monte." We walk into the building, but it's not an apartment building. It's a hospital. We're in the reception area. My mother is at the front desk, talking to a woman behind the counter. I'm behind her, and with me, to my left, is my cousin Assunta, Rachel's daughter. And we are joined by my grandmother and my aunt Roseann.

My mother says to the woman at the desk, "I'm here for Rachel. I want her to have the best. My sister will have the best of the best." The woman starts to give my mother a hard time—I don't hear the words—and she responds by putting her hands on the counter and saying, "Listen. You don't know who you're dealing with. I'm very well-known here. I'm telling you my sister will have the best of the best."

My mother walks around the desk and says to me, "Come with me. Hurry up. I want to show you something." We get in an elevator, and the doors open to a scene more beautiful than anything I could imagine. There's a hill, with beautiful, lush trees and the most vibrant green meadows. There is something that looks like a fountain with water that seems to spray up, then evaporate. "See, Johnny," my mother says, "it's beautiful here. It's really, really beautiful." Then she says, "Hurry up and go tell everyone." And as she says this, I feel as if I'm being pulled back. "Go tell everyone," she repeats, her voice sounding more and more distant until she disappears.

Soon after that dream, Aunt Rachel was admitted to Long Island's North Shore University Hospital. She was in a cancer center at the hospital called the Don Monte Pavillion. I realized that this was why my mother had pointed to the word "Monte" as we passed the Monte Excelsior apartment building. (Excelsior, by the way, means "higher" or "upward.") When I visited my aunt in the hospital, I saw that the front desk and reception area were the same ones I had seen in my dream.

I believe my mother was trying to show us that while Rachel was terminally ill, she was going to be all right once she crossed over. She was assuring us that she would take care of Rachel when she got to the Other Side—her sister would have "the best of the best." She was also using the opportunity to show me—and urge me to spread the word—that it is beautiful on the Other Side.

As you're seeing throughout this book, my mother is a great communicator, a wonderful facilitator of information. She has been "talking" about the beauty of the Other Side from the moment she arrived there. In fact, she began even *before* she got there. It happened about two hours before she completed her journey. Having been semi-comatose for days, she called out to another of her sisters and said, "Theresa, it's *so* beautiful there."

I believe that my mother knew that Theresa in particular needed to hear this. Theresa was Uncle Carmine's wife, and his fatal heart attack, which made her a widow before she was fifty, left her bitter and angry. Who could blame her? She and Carmine were both in the prime of their lives, and then—just like that—he was gone. Theresa didn't put much stock in all this "Other Side" stuff. "When you're dead you're only a picture in a frame," she was heard to say more than once. Hearing references to cemeteries and graves bothered her tremendously. "When you're dead, you're dead," she'd say. It left her with a cold feeling about Carmine, and that was truly sad. So the fact that it was specifically Theresa my mother called out to—not me, not her mother, not the group of relatives in general—was significant. My mother had not spoken in days!

In the years since Rachel's last months, when my mother showed me the Other Side as a place of pretty hills, meadows, and fountains, I've wondered if that scene meant that this is literally what it looks like on the Other Side. Or was it, like so much of what comes through, meant symbolically, using images I would understand to represent the idea that the Other Side is a place of peace and beauty, where we return to the presence of God. None of us, of course, will know until we get there. But one thing I'm sure about is that we will all get there.

My experience during Aunt Rachel's final hours provides further insight into the soul's journey. Rachel had always been very spooked by all this "psychic stuff," especially the part about the Other Side. She was afraid of what I did, and so in a funny way she was afraid of me. "Oh, those eyes, those eyes," she would always say to me. "Your eyes see into other worlds, and I can't handle that." But in the final stages of her illness, just before she slipped into unconsciousness under heavy medication, one of the last things she said was, "I'm not afraid of Johnny anymore."

Yet, when I saw her in the hospital, I felt that she *was* afraid to die. By this I mean that her soul's energy was afraid to let go. Her daughter Assunta came over to me and asked if there was anything we could do for her. "She's afraid to go," I told my cousin as her mother lay in a coma. "Can you let her know it's okay to go and that she'll be okay?" I asked. At this, I felt that our grandmother, who had passed just twelve days before, was in the room with us. I also felt my mother's presence, though she seemed to be more in the background. "You've got to tell her it's okay to go," I repeated to my cousin, knowing it had to come from her, not me. "You've got to almost walk her through this. Tell her not to be afraid."

It was early in the afternoon, and I had to leave for a series of readings at home, planning to return to the hospital later. I got to my car and headed off, and as I exited the highway a half hour later, I saw an image I'll never forget. It was such an obvious metaphor for what I was leaving behind at the hospital that it may be the most direct and clearest message I have ever gotten. And it was just the beginning.

I was shown my aunt in an airport, waiting to board a flight. She was nervous, as if afraid to fly. Her family was there, and she was looking at them, but not really connecting with them. Just looking at them, with this I-don't-want-to-go look on her face.

A while later, I was doing a reading in my house when I was interrupted by another image. This time, my aunt was at the boarding gate, but she was crying with my mother. With that, I got an over-whelming feeling of her energies being pulled to the Other Side, al-most against her will. She wasn't ready to go. It hit me so hard that when I finished the reading, I called Ellen and asked her to cancel the rest of my afternoon's appointments. I had to go back to the hospital. As I hung up, I got yet another image. This time, I was on the plane with my aunt. She was still very nervous. She was fastening her seat belt.

Driving back to the hospital, the next flash: I'm off the plane and the doors are closing. I'm seeing my aunt through the windows of the plane. She's trying to make eye contact with me, as if asking, "Am I okay?" And I'm shaking my head up and down. "Yes, you are," I said. "You're okay."

The images had started several hours before, and now they were coming fast. As I pulled into the hospital parking garage, I saw the plane on the runway. I started to run toward the hospital entrance, and as I did I saw the plane poised to take off. When I got to her room, which was filled with family, I knew immediately that a turning point had come. The energy in the room felt much more positive than when I had left. "She's feeling better," I said to my cousin Assunta. "I don't feel like she's as afraid now. I feel like my mother's here with Grandma. I feel like they're all here, getting ready to help her cross over."

Assunta asked me how close I thought she was. I looked at the clock. It was 7:30. "She'll be across by eight o'clock," I said. "The doctor said the same thing," she said. Even as we spoke, I saw the jet heading down the runway, going faster and faster and faster, and then spontaneously—though I hadn't told anyone what I was seeing—everyone in the room joined hands in prayer and said the rosary.

Rachel took her last breath at 7:59.

There is an interesting coda to this story. A few months after Rachel died, *Newsday*, the daily newspaper on Long Island, did a cover story about me in its Sunday lifestyle magazine section. "Is John Edward Communicating with the Dead?" was the headline. When I looked at the cover for the first time, I saw my aunt's face and heard her voice: *Your eyes, your eyes.* And when I opened to the story, I saw that it was illustrated by a repeated image of my eyes: four photographic slits showing only my eyes. I like to think it was my aunt's way of saying hello.

I don't impose my beliefs on anyone, and I encourage everyone I meet to make up their own minds about the essential elements of our existence. That said, my work has led me to a few beliefs. And I stress that they are beliefs—faith—because I don't know for sure. I believe, based on my experience with the spirit world, that we decide to come here. We decide when and where and why. I believe that our souls are constantly going back and forth between this side and the Other Side. We come here to learn lessons—to create opportunities to work out issues that we might have developed with people we've been with in past lives, and to work out debits and credits of those relationships. This is also known as karma.

We don't know what these lessons are on a conscious level, but the soul knows. The soul has memory. In my readings I don't bring up past lives because I feel that's what they are: past. They happened, you learned from them or not, and now you're in this life. The time for evaluation of the previous life is in what Brian Weiss, in *Many Lives, Many Masters,* calls "the in-between state." It's not unlike the movie *Defending Your Life.* When you get to the Other Side, you must review your life and incorporate it into your plan for your existence on the Other Side and maybe for the next incarnation. We are not punished on the Other Side, except by ourselves. We ask ourselves why we did what we did, and seek to improve.

An example is suicide. I've had people come through who have ended their own lives, and in some cases they have given me the feeling that they have a spiritual type of therapy going on around them. Even though they are all right—they are not in any kind of limbo, as some might believe—they are trying to understand why they did what they did, and using it in learning their spiritual lessons. There is also a sense of sorrow for the people they left behind. This is not to say such feelings are unique to those who have committed suicide. I have had many spirits who passed from the physical state in "natural" ways, or in accidents, come through conveying to me that they are working on those same kinds of lessons. What matters is how they spent their time on this side. Someone with minimal human success—spiritual, not material, of course—will have to work on his lessons on the Other Side. Our physical lives are analogous to formal schooling. You're better off doing well in school—you'll have a leg up when you graduate—but even if you don't do well, or you drop out (suicide), you can still become a success story. It depends on what you do after you leave school.

Trying to use spirit messages to "read" a spirit's situation has led me to follow Rule Number One about spirit communication: There are no rules. For instance, I have had heard from spirits of people who have been murdered, and they have been angry. They were not ready to go. But others have come through as very loving and contented. They didn't care how they died. They had completed their lessons. Although I don't encounter them personally—my guides keep them out—I believe that there are also what are called "earthbound" energies—those that have not made the transition successfully and are in a kind of limbo. These spirits still care about material and earthly things—unlike spirits who have reached the Other Side.

I have been asked how long we stay on the Other Side before returning. Will someone who's been gone, say, fifty years, come through, or will his spirit already have returned to a new physical body? First, I think souls do not return to earth that quickly. It's also my feeling that the concept of time is ours—not theirs. So I think it's entirely possible to connect with spirits going back decades, perhaps even centuries, though they would presumably have no reason to connect with someone they never knew and who can't validate who they are.

Before we come back to this side, we connect with a spirit who will be our Master Guide. In essence, we say, "Cover me, I'm going in." And our Master Guide will look after us from the Other Side as we pursue the lessons we've decided we need to learn in this life, from its beginning to its end. When we have learned those lessons, we are ready to return to the Other Side.

We have other spirit guides besides our Master Guide, and I call them secondary or tertiary guides. It's my impression that they change throughout our lives, depending on what we're doing. If you decide to become a doctor, there will be a spirit guide who will help you be a better doctor. But what you do with that help is the key. We have free will, and it's our job to use this help in positive ways. What of the doctor who is bad at his work? Even failure may be part of the plan because it allows a lesson to be learned. That's why I got the image of the great college hall. We are here to learn lessons.

Who are these "secondary and tertiary" guides? For one thing, they are evolved souls who are also very *in*volved. Sometimes they can be related to us, as in the case of Andrew and his great-grandfather. And sometimes their guidance is direct and very personal, helping us learn our lessons.

I did a reading once for a man who had lost his younger brother. The family was extremely wealthy—oozing money—and the younger brother, call him Jonathan, hadn't had to work a day in his life. He lived life fast—fast cars, exotic travel, lots of women, drugs. A classic spoiled rich kid who never had to grow up. And, not surprisingly, he died the same way—drugged up while driving. Now, Jonathan's older brother was with me for a reading. And Jonathan came through, told me about his life, and described how his brother's son was following in his footsteps—living fast and loose, his parents unable to control him. Jonathan wanted his brother to know that he was sorry for the way he had lived, and that he was determined to help guide his nephew to a better path. What I think he was trying to say was that by working with his nephew, he was working off his own energy— working on his own issues, belatedly and from the Other Side, as well as trying to guide his nephew.

I don't mean to imply that when our relatives die they automatically become our spirit guides, that they're watching over us and directing the show. That's a common misconception. I'm constantly asked by people who have had experiences with after-death communication from loved ones if their friends and relatives are there all the time, watching out for them. They are there, they may be close, but it doesn't mean they are your own personal spirit guides.

In one reading, I told a woman that her brother was saying that he had come through to one of her young children—a niece who was born several years after he passed to the Other Side. She asked me if that meant he was her spirit guide. Not necessarily, I told her. More than likely it was just a visit, maybe a way for him to give her a feeling of him, as an act of love for you. This began an interesting conversation about visits, especially where it concerns children.

"She's only five," the woman said. "How would she know that he was 'visiting?' "

"She might, though," I said. "She might have been able to sense his energy, see him, feel him, hear him, without realizing what was happening. Children are very open. And so are older people."

"Well, it's interesting, because recently my daughter said something very odd. We were driving and she was in the back seat with her twin sister. She started describing how sometimes she sees faces dropping down from the sky. Lots of faces, and some seemed like good people and some bad. And then her sister said, 'Only Allie can see it,' as if they'd had this conversation before, like, 'Do you ever see these faces?' "

"Well, let me tell you," I said, "my grandmother used to say the same thing. She used to say that she saw faces in her bedroom at night, coming in and staring at her. I'd say, 'Grandma's cracking up.' But Grandma only said that on the nights that I did readings. This was when I was younger, living at home, and I did readings upstairs. And many times we could correlate what she was seeing to my readings. The morning after a reading, she'd say, 'Johnny, I saw these faces last night,' and I could tell which reading that was connected to."

"What do you think she was doing?"

"I think she was able to connect and see the energies. I believe they know who they can show themselves to. I think they can tell from our energies who can perceive *their* energies, and in which manner to show them."

After my mother died, someone asked me if she was one of my spirit guides. "I certainly hope not," I said.

"Why not?" I was asked.

"Let's put it this way. My mother's only over there a couple of years. I want somebody guiding me who has a hell of a lot more experience than she does. No offense to her, but mother or not, I want my guides to be advanced."

A few years later, I was asked the same question by someone else. But this time, I had to concede a point. "What if your mother *is* advanced? If it's a cycle, if you are reincarnated many times and you keep evolving, maybe your mother has evolved very highly by now."

That may well be true. But now I see that it's almost beside the point. Whether she is a spirit guide to me or not, I know my mother hasn't left me.

" 'N O W   H E ' S   Y O U R   O L D E R   B R O T H E R' '

F ew experiences have been more personally intriguing for me than the one
I am about to describe. I bring it up here for
a few reasons: one, because it relates to the
importance of a person's openness to psychic energy; and two, because it shows how
people come to these experiences from many
different angles and preconceptions and react to it in varying ways. It's also another
great example of the endlessly fascinating
ways in which spiritual energies come
through and sometimes converge.

It was a March morning, shortly before
daybreak, and I was jarred out of sleep by
a voice that shouted, "John, wake up!" I
bolted upright and looked around, wondering, at first, if someone was in the house. It
was dark, and Sandra was sleeping beside
me. *Who was that?* I thought, quickly realizing I had heard this telepathically. Whoever it was, this spirit was powerful. It
wanted my attention and got it, showing me
a single, compelling piece of information:

17

This was a person, a young man, who had been hit over the head with a baseball bat.

"Sandra," I said, nudging my wife. "Wake up. Who do we know who was hit over the head with a baseball bat?" It seemed to me that a spirit so pushy that it would come into my bedroom and wake me up had to be someone I knew. "What?" Sandra asked, dazed and half asleep. I repeated the question, "Who do we know who was hit with a bat? Someone just woke me up, someone who was hit with a baseball bat." Sandra said she didn't know anyone who'd been hit on the head with a bat and went back to sleep. I spent half the morning calling people in my family and asking the same question: Who do we know who was killed by a blow to the head with a baseball bat? No one I called had a clue.

I had three readings scheduled that night, starting at six o'clock. The first two were fairly routine—some good information, some vague. The third and last was a woman around forty, with thick, dark hair and a wide smile indicating a very open person. Her name was Randi. She sat down, and when I asked her if I could hold onto something of hers, she gave me her watch.

The first thing that came through was a male, a father figure. "He's telling me he died of cancer," I told Randi.

She shook her head. "I don't know who that would be," she said.

"Yes, you do," I said. "He's coming through very strongly."

"No," Randi insisted. "My father's alive. My stepfather's alive."

We weren't off to a good start. I was annoyed that she was failing to acknowledge information I knew was right. "No. I'll stand by this," I said. "He says your mother was bossy. He's showing me the initial S."

Suddenly, Randi's eyes widened. "Oh!" she said. "Sidney! He was my mother's last husband! He died of cancer two years ago. Yes, she can be bossy."

"Psychic amnesia?" I remarked. (I define psychic amnesia as the instantaneous and complete deterioration of a client's brain, rendering her incapable of remembering who she is, who she's related to and how they died, usually accompanied by an irresistible urge to respond "no" to all statements made by the medium.)

"They got together after I was out of college," Randi said. "I never considered him a father figure. But I guess *he* did." She laughed with embarrassment at her oversight. She joked about whether it was possible to insult a spirit. And would there be consequences?

"Now they're showing me, like 'ten-ten,' " I went on. "Two tens. Anyone significant have a birthday in October, the tenth month? Or the tenth day of a month?" Randi thought for a moment. It didn't ring any bells. It was coming through more insistently now, but Randi was just as insistent that no one she knew had an October birthday. I moved on.

"You have a son?" I asked.

"Yes."

"He's starting school in September?"

"He starts kindergarten then."

"They're showing me that. They're showing me it in relation to another event. They're showing me cancer and indicating someone above you: mother, father, aunt, uncle. I would take that to mean that someone might be diagnosed at the same time your son starts school."

I saw a worried look on Randi's face. "The cancer has nothing to do with my son?" she asked, looking for assurance.

"No. It's someone above you. They're showing me your son going to school just as a reference point."

"So it could be one of my parents."

"Could be." I told her that I have a simple rule: While I don't want to cause anyone needless worry, I always pass on the information I am given because I am only given information that I am meant to pass on. In a case like this, it might mean the information is intended to help: either to prepare or to warn. But I also told her that it is always possible that I am misunderstanding or misinterpreting a message. "When's your son's birthday?" I asked.

"July eighth."

"Okay, he's a Cancer."

"So am I."

"Okay, so it might be just an acknowledgment of birthdays."

Now I saw the "10" again. Someone was showing me a "10," then another "10." It was very strong: "10-10." I looked at Randi: Anything? Nothing.

I refocused, and brought in another male figure. I heard a "J" name; it sounded like Jack—no, more like Jacques. "My grandfather was Jacques," Randi said. I gave myself a secret high-five. I love nailing unusual names. So often names come through so fast that I only get an initial, or maybe the general sound. "Okay, he's acknowledging you," I said. "And he says he's with somebody. Rob. You know him as Robby."

"Yes, my brother," Randi said. She looked as though I had hit a raw nerve, but she was working hard to control her excitement, as if she had resolved to maintain her skepticism and reserve judgment.

Now I felt a sharp, blunt pain at the back of my head. Then, in the next instant, it hit me like a thunderbolt: "Oh my God," I blurted, "this guy was hit with a baseball bat! And he woke me up this morning!" I knew it was the same spirit. It had that same feeling.

"At five o'clock this morning," I explained excitedly, "I heard this voice call out, 'Rob, wake up!' I bolted out of bed. At first I thought someone was in the house. Then I realized it was a spirit, and I saw that it was someone who was hit by a baseball bat." I told her how I'd called my relatives asking if we knew anyone who'd been hit over the head with a baseball bat. "Now I know, this is the guy! It's your brother." I found it exhilarating to think that a spirit might have been so anxious about connecting with someone that he barged in and woke me up a full twelve hours before his sister was scheduled to come for her reading.

That in itself is not what made this episode unique. It was what Randi said next. "This is so strange," she said. "I had a dream about your mother this morning, about the same time this happened to you. This woman was shrouded in smoke."

"My mother died of lung cancer," I confirmed. "She was a heavy smoker."

How did she know it was my mother? She didn't know either me or my mother. She just knew it, she told me later. The way you just know things in dreams. It made perfect sense to me. Dreams are a primary venue for spirit communication, especially for people who are tuned in to psychic forces. But I couldn't deny that I found the intersecting events remarkable, the fact that *my* spirits showed up in *her* dream. And at the very same time her brother was waking me up. "It wasn't just a dream," I told Randi. "It was a visit." I thanked her for it, leaving my own emotions aside for the moment.

I got back to Randi's brother, Robby. He told me that he didn't see the fatal blow coming. He was hit from behind, he showed me. He conveyed that his spirit left right away, but his body remained for a little while. "He was connected to life-support machines for a day," Randi confirmed.

"He wants you to know that he's fine," I said. "He's with Jacques and also with . . . sounds like Helen. They were there to greet him when he crossed over."

"Helen was our grandmother, Jacques' wife," Randi said. She was taking copious notes. I saw that she wrote down the three names I had given her, all underlined three times.

Robby was telling me that he was Randi's older brother. But when I reported this, she shook her head. In fact, she said, he was nine years *younger* than her. "He was only eighteen when he died," she said. "I was really like a second mother to him."

"Well, for some reason he's telling me he's your older brother."

Now Robby was showing me an item of clothing. "He's showing me something of his that you have," I said. "A jacket. No, a sweat-shirt." Randi nodded. "Well, actually I have both a jacket and a sweatshirt that were his. They're the only things I have."

"He says he's come to you before."

"I know that," Randi said. "I've felt that."

"Now, you have three children. Two girls and a boy."

"That's right."

"He's also come to one of them. The one with the big eyes—Katie."

"Oh my God," Randi said, losing her composure for the first time. "I do have a daughter named Katie. She *is* the one with the big eyes." Then she laughed. "I'm not surprised she's the one he would come to. She's the one who sometimes needs a little extra guidance, shall we say."

Now Robby came back to something from a little earlier. Again, he told me he was older than Randi. But then I realized what he was trying to say: that *now* he was her older brother. Spirits are highly evolved entities, I explained to her, so that in terms of spiritual knowledge and wisdom, her baby brother had far surpassed her. She smiled serenely at the thought.

Randi's reading lasted more than two hours, more than twice as long as typical. Actually, it evolved into a visit, a conversation. I felt connected to her because my mother had chosen to visit me through her. In effect, she was acting as a medium for me. As I've said, my mother has passed messages to me through other professional mediums. What had never happened was for her to visit through an otherwise typical Tuesday night appointment. Each of us has some psychic ability. Randi might have had more than most.

She had arrived at my door that evening in early March after a series of events that prove the old adage that some things are just meant to be. For me, that is not just a cliché. It means that while we all have free will, it is frequently guided by what might be called "spirit will." I have seen time and again how spirits make things happen. Why did Randi come to me? It wasn't just about her. And it wasn't just about me.

Once in a while, I like to talk to clients after a particularly intriguing encounter to fill in the blanks of their stories. Doing a reading, I sometimes feel like a detective, or a contestant in a game of "I've Got a Secret." A spirit might come through as some sort of riddler. So whether it is plain curiosity or a desire to deepen my understanding of the spirit world and help become better at my job, I have on a few occasions debriefed clients, saying, in effect, "Now tell me the whole story." In so doing I also sometimes learn about the factors that led to a person's point of view about spirit communication: did he or she come as a believer, a nonbeliever, or somewhere in between? Why do they feel the way they do? How did his or her spouse feel about it? And how, if at all, did the experience change them? Often, people tell me these things without my asking. And as you may have guessed by now, some have elaborated, at my request, so I could relate their stories in some detail in this book. Randi's story is one of those cases—at once unique and universal.

It had started for her one night in December 1995, when a friend named Alexandra came over to dinner and told her about a psychic reading she had had with "this guy named John Edward" who had connected her with her dead relatives. Randi was what I consider a healthy skeptic. She was a biologist by profession, someone not given to blind faith and who insisted on hard proof in her own work. But she was not a cynic. In fact, she believed in psychic phenomena and felt that she had experienced it herself at different times in her life. She just didn't believe everything she heard, and assumed that many who advertised themselves as psychics or mediums were either frauds or people who took advantage of the current interest in spirit communication by exaggerating a limited ability. Her husband, Peter, meanwhile, thought it was all a bunch of hooey.

Alexandra told Randi and Peter that she had first seen me at a lecture a few months before. A friend had brought her, and she had found a couple of moments that night especially compelling. One was when I connected a woman in the audience with her son, a young man who had been killed in a car accident. He was telling me that his mother had been unable to go on with her life, that she carried his ID bracelet with her at all times, and he wanted her to stop. "He says there's no need to keep carrying this bracelet around with you," I told the mother. "If you put it away, that will be the start of your healing process. He says he's all right and that you should let go. It's okay." The woman began to sob. She went into her pocketbook and pulled out a bracelet with her son's name engraved on it.

Alexandra, intrigued, made an appointment to see me for a private reading, and I conveyed much information that she confirmed: that her mother's father was an alcoholic, and that her mother had been raised in an orphanage, where a certain nun had taken care of her. The source of this information was Alexandra's grandfather, the alcoholic, who had passed of liver disease many years before. "He wants you to tell your mother that he's sorry, he did the best he could," I told Alexandra. I also told her that she and her husband would soon be going a far distance (it felt like Russia) to complete a transaction, though it wasn't a business deal. I had the feeling it was going to be an adoption. She confirmed this, saying they had indeed filed an adoption application with a Russian agency just six weeks before. I also told her that she had a young person in her home at the moment, whom they were just helping out. He was not going to stay long. For several weeks, in fact, a parentless teenager had been staying with them. Alexandra's husband, a lawyer, had represented the boy pro bono in a minor criminal situation (a modern Jean Valjean, he had been caught stealing tofu from a convenience store) and he and Alexandra had taken him in temporarily to get him on his feet.

Alexandra had come into the reading unaware of some of the key information I delivered to her about her mother and grandfather. But when she called her mother and told her what she had heard—especially details about her father, the orphanage, and the nun—her mother broke down and cried. At first, Alexandra had considered the possibility that I was "mind reading." But the fact that I had conveyed so much information that she didn't know, until her mother confirmed it, convinced her that this was real. That her grandfather had come through.

When Randi and Peter heard all this, they didn't know what to make of it. Peter, a writer, was fascinated, and also a bit flustered. He had never believed in the spirit world or any kind of hereafter, and had always operated under the assumption that death was The End. Alexandra's story flew in the face of his whole concept of life and death. And he couldn't just dismiss it. Here was an intelligent, credible, professional woman, a good friend whose feet were firmly planted on the earth, sitting in his dining room and relating a catalog of details about her life that were supposedly being passed on from "spirits" who were eager to establish their presence. Whoever they were, he agreed, they were dead-on accurate.

Peter later told me, "This whole thing spooked me. It would be one thing if you were a superb mind reader; I was open to the remote possibility that some people are gifted with extraordinary, inexplicable psychic ability. But Alex was saying these were messages, conversations, with dead people. I wanted no part of it. I certainly had no intention of ever visiting such a person. Why ask for trouble?"

That night, Randi later told me, she and Peter kicked around the possibilities with Alexandra and her husband, Rob. Could this be some sort of trick? Some sort of psychological sleight of hand? Peter acknowledged that there was a big part of him that wanted to believe. He had grown up with a considerable fear of death. It would be nice to find out his worries were unnecessary. For now, though, he had no interest in thinking any more about it.

Randi, meanwhile, announced that she wanted to come for her own reading. She'd had only one previous experience with a psychic, and it had not been a good one. It was over the phone, with someone in California who came recommended. At one point, Randi mentioned to him that she had a religious goblet that had belonged to her brother. When her mother spoke to the man separately, he told her, "I see a goblet." So Randi had her eyes wide open. But so was her mind. She had long been curious about spirit communication, and it was for a particular reason that she hoped I was legitimate. Twelve years before, Randi's eighteen-year-old brother, Robby, was murdered. He was spending New Year's Day in a video arcade on the Upper East Side of Manhattan when a pair of young thugs came in with a baseball bat and announced they were looking for someone named Dennis. "Who's gonna stop us?" one of them demanded. He looked right at Robby. "Not me," he said, putting up his hands. He turned to leave. Without warning, the other one slammed the bat over Robby's head. He collapsed to the floor, his skull crushed. The next day, brain-dead, Robby was disconnected from life-support. Randi was devastated, especially because she and her little brother were so close. She had carried his death with her every one of the four thousand days since, almost as if she had lost her own child.

Over the years, Randi told me, she had felt Robby's presence. Not constantly, not even often, but at certain times she had felt he was there with her, and that he wanted her to know it. The first and most dramatic time was not long after his death. "I was sitting at my desk at home, about three months after he died, so I was still thinking about him all the time," she relates. "I know it's hard to believe"— I find almost nothing hard to believe—"but all of a sudden, a spider plant that was hanging from the ceiling, in front of a window, began swinging wildly back and forth. I mean wildly. It was still winter so the windows were closed and there was no air conditioning on. I looked for a heat source but couldn't find any. Finally, I said simply, 'Hi, Robby.' And it stopped."

That incident, which was also experienced, independently, by her mother, shaped Randi's concept of the Other Side. Previously, she had lived under the working theory that perhaps we leave behind energies when we die, and that for unexplained reasons some of us have an ability to tap into these vestigial vibrations. But the incident with the plant suggested to her that there was more to it, that we do go on living in another form, and that the energies are "live" and the communication is interactive. She felt comfortable with these possibilities and had no strong desire to explore it further. Until now. Alexandra's story piqued her interest, and the more she thought about it, the more she wanted to connect with her brother in a more concrete way than through the symbol of a swinging spider plant.

Robby had died on New Year's Day, and the anniversary was fast approaching. Randi badly wanted to come for a reading around that time, partly out of sentiment, partly because she thought it might be a time when he was more likely to be around her.

Still, the road to connecting with Robby was a long and winding one—guided, it seems, by something more than simple earthly desire. Randi put herself on my waiting list for a private reading and waited for a call back. And waited. And called again. And, I'm sorry to say, waited some more. What happened next shows how powerful and determined life forces can be.

One night in January, Sandra and I were out to dinner with a couple we knew through dance competitions. We were finishing our meal when a woman stopped at our table to say hello to the people we were with, whom she apparently knew through a business connection. After some pleasantries, our dining companions introduced the woman to Sandra and me. An almost shocked look crossed the woman's face when she saw me. She obviously recognized me, though I couldn't place her.

"We've met," she said. "I don't know if you remember me, but I had a reading with you a couple of months ago." It was Alexandra. I would later learn that the reason she was so taken aback was that she and her husband had just finished dinner with Randi and Peter— right on the other side of a high-backed booth—and that among other things, they had been talking about *me*, joking at one point about how hard it was to get an appointment with a medium these days. (Some psychic I am; I had no idea I was the topic of discussion right at the next table. In fact, I had literally been sitting back-to-back with Randi. All I can say is: I *told* you I can turn it on and off. I was just trying to have dinner.)

Alexandra dashed to the coatroom and brought Randi back. Somewhat sheepishly, Randi told me she hadn't been able to get through for an appointment, at which point Sandra offered some assistance. "Write your number down," she said. "I'll make sure you get a call back." I looked at my wife quizzically. "Psychic stage mother," I said. But the fact was that I'd never seen Sandra do something like that. We hadn't been married that long and she was still getting used to my line of work. She made a point of staying out of medium business. When I asked her about it, she said she had no idea why she did it.

After the weekend, Sandra gave Randi's number to my assistant, Ellen, but apparently it got mixed in with a lot of other numbers and failed to yield a quick appointment. "I got tired of waiting," Randi told me later. "So I made other arrangements. Another friend of mine had gone to a medium and she'd had a good reading and recommended him. I was really anxious to connect with my brother so I decided to forget about you and go to him. So I made an appointment, but when I came for my reading, the guy seemed all jumpy. We sat down and he said a few things that were very vague, but he was obviously having trouble. He wasn't getting anything. Finally, he explained that the person before me had really bad karma and that he couldn't read me and I had to leave. So I left. I went home shaking my head, thinking maybe this just wasn't meant to be. Two days later, I get a call saying you had a cancellation and asking if I could come in the next night. And the next morning, I had the dream about your mother."

It was raining hard when Randi kissed her children goodnight and headed out for our eight o'clock appointment. She'd carried the dream around with her all day. She assumed it was because she was so excited about finally having a reading. She was about to discover that there was more to it than that; that this was not just a dream but a firsthand encounter with the Other Side. I, meanwhile, was about to discover the identity of the young man who'd been hit over the head with a baseball bat then woken me up to tell me about it.

What about Peter? As I said, this wasn't just about Randi. When she got home that night, her husband was practically pacing. She'd been gone nearly three hours. "I was worried," Peter recounted. "This was taking awfully long. Again, I was spooked by this. It was fine if Randi wanted to do it; I understood her reasons, and if I were her I probably would have felt the same way. But the more time passed, the more I worried about what was going on. 'Who is this guy, anyway? Most of these psychics are just fakes, scammers, right? What nonsense was she being fed? Was she getting bad news? What if she had been told something upsetting, and she'd had an accident driving home?' You know the old cliché about fearing the unknown. I actually called Alexandra to ask how long these things usually take. And of course she told me hers lasted less than an hour.

"When she finally came home, Randi had a strange look on her face—not upset, not excited, just sort of . . . touched. Like she'd been through something deeply affecting and she needed some time to let it sink in. This sounds very silly, but she had this dizzy, almost smitten look. Anyway, the first thing she said was that the medium had told her that a member of our family in the generation above us was going to get cancer in the fall. I don't know why she chose this as the first thing to tell me, but I was enraged. All my ambivalence and cynicism came spilling out: 'That's why I didn't want you to go! Who is this son of a bitch to tell you something like that? He doesn't know that! They should not tell people anything bad. This is just what I was afraid of.' I noticed how calm Randi was. 'He's not always right,' she said. 'He says that sometimes he misinterprets the messages. He says it could have something to do with someone born under the cancer sign.' There was a lot more, she said. She told me to just calm down and she'd tell me all about it. She takes out this yellow legal pad filled with detailed notes. And she tells me this astonishing story about Robby. I was completely amazed about the details—how could you know that he'd been killed by a baseball bat? And all these names. You didn't call out five or six before you hit on the right one. It was just like that—'Jacques.' 'Helen.' 'The one with the big eyes—Katie.' 'Rob—you know him as Robby.' "

Peter said he and Randi found the reading so accurate that they wondered whether it was all a setup. They had a conversation I'm sure is not unusual among skeptical, intelligent people encountering legitimate spirit communication for the first time. "Peter and several of our disbelieving friends wondered if you could have researched this somehow," Randi recalls. "But I had only given my first name and phone number when I'd made the appointment. The phone is listed in Peter's name, which is different from mine. I use my maiden name. For that matter, even my maiden name is different from Robby's and my grandparents because we were technically half-siblings. Theoretically, you could have looked up newspaper stories about Robby's murder, but how would you know about the jacket and the sweatshirt? And all this research for a hundred dollars?"

The next day, Randi called her mother in California to tell her about what had happened. She recapped the highlights, then told her about the one loose end of the reading: the insistent spirit that kept chiming in with "10-10." "Mom," she asked, "does '10-10' mean anything to you?"

"Of course," her mother said. "October 10th. That was Sidney's birthday." Sidney was her mother's late husband, "the father figure" that Randi didn't recognize at first. "Oh, no, poor Sidney," Randi told her mother. "The poor guy was just jumping up and down, hoping for some acknowledgment."

A few weeks later, Randi noticed an old Army photo of Sidney propped up on a bookcase in her den. She had no idea how it had gotten there.

Meanwhile, Peter mulled over the situation and ultimately decided that the only way he could figure out if he believed or not was to go for a reading himself. I should note here that by the time he called for an appointment, the cancer prediction that came in Randi's reading for someone in the generation above had unfortunately been confirmed. Sometime after Randi's reading, Peter's mother was diagnosed with breast cancer, though happily it was caught early. Whether I was right about the timing is not clear. The cancer was not diagnosed in the fall, as I had indicated, coinciding with Peter and Randi's son starting school, but some six months later. However, it is possible she actually "got" the cancer in the fall, since she had a clean mammography not long before that.

In any event, Peter was now looking to get his own firsthand experience. What follows is based on his notes of the reading.

I started by hearing a name that had an "R-T" sound to it. "Who's 'R-T'?" I asked Peter. It might have been a Ruth or Rita.

Peter said it could be his father's name, Robert.

"It has an out-of-state feel," I said. "And it's connected to an 'E.' Who's 'E'?"

"My mother's name is Elaine. She and my father spend their winters in Florida. But I doubt that's it. They're up here now. They're only down there four months of the year."

"Boca Raton?"

"Right."

"The spirits don't like to be challenged," I said with a smile.

I told Peter that it was a male figure who was coming through with this information, and he was acknowledging the "R-T" and the "E." He was also showing me two red roses, indicating an anniversary. But one seemed to be for the "R-T" and "E" and the other for Peter himself. "Whoever this is is saying that they, the 'R-T' and the 'E,' have an important occasion that's close to an important occasion for you," I explained.

"Well, my parents' anniversary is March twenty-seventh. My anniversary is March twenty-fifth," Peter said.

"He's giving me the name Samuel," I said now. It was very clear.

"My grandfather was Samuel."

"He's showing me specifically Samuel, not Sam," I said, stretching my hands apart, as if pulling taffy, to signify the longer version.

"Yeah, he did not like being called Sam. He always signed his name 'Samuel,' even on personal letters."

Now Peter's grandfather was showing me a piano. When I told him this, Peter acknowledged it enthusiastically. He later told me that he came from a very musical background, and a piano is one of the strongest symbols in his family—something his grandfather would definitely show me to validate his presence. "My mother and father met as music majors in college," he said. "On Saturday nights, they would go to the music department of Brooklyn College to play piano duets. And my grandfather, though a painter by vocation, arranged and conducted a small orchestra on the side. One of the strongest images of my youth is of my grandfather coming out from the city on the weekends and arranging music at the baby grand piano we had in our house."

Now I started hearing music, two different kinds of music, and I was seeing two pianos and feeling like one was meant for Peter's father. I interpreted this to mean that Peter's grandfather was trying to show me that there was a difference in their styles. "Like your father plays a bouncier style," I said.

"That's true," I said. "My grandfather was classical, my father plays mostly jazz."

"Your grandfather wants you to know he's fine."

"Is he saying anything about my grandmother? Is she there with him?"

"I'm not getting anything. Sorry. But that doesn't mean she's not there or she's not fine. There's really no way to know why they come through with what they come through with. And there's always the possibility I'm missing something. But your grandfather is saying that he's proud of your accomplishments."

Now I felt the presence of someone who passed around the time Peter was in college; maybe right after college.

"Still my grandfather?" Peter asked. "He died about a year after I graduated."

"He thanks you for what you wrote about him."

"I don't think I wrote anything about my grandfather. Wait a minute. It could be someone else. Keep going."

"Did he wear bow ties? He's showing me someone wearing a bow tie."

"The person I'm thinking of didn't wear bow ties, as far as I remember."

The person I was seeing was a bit nerdy looking, but I didn't want to put it that way. "Was he kind of awkward looking?" I asked.

"No," Peter said. "Actually he was kind of impressive looking."

"Hold on—I know what it is now," I said. "He's showing me Les Nessman, a character on the TV show *WKRP in Cincinnati*. Remember that show?" I explained that spirits give me a lot of pop culture references, especially TV shows, because they know that's what I know; they do this to give me an image I will understand. "So why's he showing me Les Nessman?"

Peter thought a few seconds, then said, "Wasn't Les Nessman the newsman on that show? This makes sense. It all fits." Peter was excited. "The person I'm thinking of was my mentor in journalism school, in Ohio. *WKRP in Cincinnati*—Cincinnati's in Ohio. He's showing you *a newsman in Ohio*. He did die just a few months after

I graduated. And when you said he thanks me for what I wrote about him, that fits too. His wife asked me to deliver one of the eulogies at his memorial service. I was working at my first newspaper job in New Jersey, and I drove all night back to Ohio for the weekend. Along the way, I wrote a tribute in longhand, in a reporter's notebook. I composed it in my head as I drove and wrote it down every time I took a break from driving. I still have it."

I felt the presence of yet another spirit. "Not to cut you off," I said, "but I'm seeing Colonel Sanders."

"Colonel Sanders?" Peter asked, chuckling. "As in Kentucky Fried Chicken? That Colonel Sanders?"

"Yes. Anyone in your family look like Colonel Sanders?"

"Got me there."

"He's acknowledging someone who's still with us, a woman. She's wearing a sweater with just the top button fastened and the rest draped over her shoulders."

"That sounds like my grandmother. She's ninety years old. She wears her sweaters exactly that way, just about every day. It's almost a trademark. But I don't know who Colonel Sanders is."

The next day, Peter visited his mother and father to tell them about the reading. He wanted to do it in person because, besides the solid hits about his grandfather and his college professor, there was as usual a lot he couldn't confirm and thought it might mean something to his parents. "When I asked about Colonel Sanders, a funny look crossed my mother's face," Peter told me later. "She went upstairs and came down with a picture of her grandfather, who I never knew. It was from my parents' wedding. It showed her grandfather walking down the aisle. He had white hair with a moustache and a white tuft on his chin. He looked just like Colonel Sanders. The woman with the sweater, my grandmother, was his daughter."

Peter says he came out of the experience with an entirely new view about what happens after we die. He no longer regarded death as eternal nonexistence, and he no longer feared it the way he had ever since he could remember. For the first time, he opened himself to life beyond what we can see and touch. I asked him what moved him most. He said that there were two things. First, there was his grandfather. "I was really hoping for him," Peter said. "He's the one I really expected because we were very close. We always shared a certain bond and though it's been over twenty years since he died, I've never stopped missing him. I always regretted that I never had the chance to know him as an adult. Just the possibility that he was coming through was a comforting thought." But while he was impressed and excited about the messages I had passed on validating his grandfather, it was the appearance of Peter's college professor that intrigued him most. "I really hadn't thought about him in a very long time," he said, "and he wasn't on the list of obvious people to come through. So the fact that he did, and that he was thanking me for my tribute to him, well, I found that terrifically moving."

A few days after the reading, Peter was jogging and found himself thinking about his professor. "If that was you," he thought as he ran, "thanks for your visit. And if it was, please come again." He was hoping for some additional validation. That weekend, Peter and Randi went out to dinner with a couple they had recently met. At one point, the woman in the couple mentioned that she had grown up in Omaha, Nebraska. "The *Omaha World-Herald*," Peter interjected for no apparent reason, then added, "It's an occupational hazard. I can't hear the name of a city without thinking of its newspaper." The woman laughed. Then her husband started poking her in the side, saying, "Tell him about that guy. Tell him about the guy on the newspaper." The woman looked at her husband, as if to say, "Why? That's not very interesting." But her husband kept prodding her, as if it was something really important. And the woman finally told Peter how the father of her best childhood friend had won a Pulitzer prize for investigative reporting while working on a weekly newspaper in Omaha.

"That's very strange," Peter said. To explain why it was strange, he had to tell her the story of our reading, specifically, the part about how his college professor had come through. "My professor, before he came to Ohio, had been the managing editor of the paper in Omaha you're talking about. It was the first time a weekly newspaper won a Pulitzer prize. He was that guy's boss." It struck Peter as odd that his professor had come up twice in a week, after being out of his everyday consciousness for so long. But this in itself is not what Peter found most intriguing. It was what the woman's husband said as the four of them took an after-dinner stroll to a nearby Starbucks. "What's really weird," he said, "is that I have no idea why I kept trying to get her to tell about that guy on the newspaper. I never do that. I never tell her what to say. But I felt this *pressure* to get her to tell you about it. I wouldn't stop until she told you that, and I have no idea why. Something was making me do that." Or maybe some-one?

THE DRUGGIST AND THE DONOR

18

When I first started this work as a teenager, people who came to me for readings would ask if I could pose specific questions to a spirit. I would say, "No, no, it doesn't work that way. You only get what they come through with." But the more I did it, the more I realized that I *can* ask questions. In fact, it's part of a good reading. I'm like a journalist interviewing the spirits, or at times like a detective trying to get to the bottom of a mystery. And sometimes, I'm Larry King, passing on questions from the listening audience to the subject.

It doesn't mean we will get the answers we want, or any answer at all. For instance, if a spirit is asked a question designed to elicit some information about the future, we might not get a response because the spirit knows that to answer will be to interfere with a life plan. But I will try. I am constantly talking to them during a reading—telepathically, not out loud—trying to draw them out. The process is unquestionably interactive. They are there with us. Or more precisely, with you. I try to make my clients understand how crucial they are to the process. Remember, I tell them, they're here for you, not me. I'm just the go-between, the guy delivering the messages. So now when someone asks if he or she can ask a question, I say, "Well, they came with you." And if a particular spirit was the focal point of a reading and it was the one a client came for, I might end the session by asking if there's anything he or she would like to ask the spirit. In most cases, we get an answer.

Many people come for just that: answers. They want to know if their loved ones suffered before they passed. Did they know how much they were loved and missed? Or, in the case of a sudden death such as a heart attack, a car accident, or a homicide, they feel an emptiness because they never had a chance to say good-bye. In still other cases, there is some sort of unfinished business. In other words, many people want that **one last time.**

Dave, in his early forties, came to me hoping to start closing a hole in his life. As he was to tell me later, he wasn't sure what he believed about life-after-death in general, and the legitimacy of mediumship in particular. But he wanted to see how a personal experience might affect his perspective. One thing was sure: It would take a lot to convince him this was real. But if he was convinced, the payoff would be great.

With my clients' permission, I had begun taping some sessions for possible use in this book. Dave's was one of them. Early in his reading, I felt a male figure coming through and pulling me upward, indicating someone above him. "Has your dad passed?" I asked. Dave said yes.

"Okay, because your dad is coming through. Did he have problems in the chest area? He's pointing to his chest."

"In the end, yes," Dave said.

"Now, was your dad away from you when he passed? Because he's showing me there's a distance, which could mean physically away, or it might have been emotional distance. But he does indicate a distance of some sort. Now your dad's talking about being here and there, here and there, here and there. Is he trying to tell me that he was in your life, he was out of your life, he was in your life, he was out of your life? Because I feel like he's here but he's not here, he's there, then he's not there. He's kind of like a phantom."

"That would be a fair statement," Dave said.

"That's how he's coming through to me. Has your mom passed?"

"No."

"Who else would be like a mother besides a mom? There's someone coming through claiming to be Mom. Unless it's a mother-in-law. But there's a female figure who's passed from congestive heart failure. Or problems in the chest area. Who is Suzanne or Susan? Who's the female 'S'? Connected to your mom's side of the family."

"Susan," Dave said.

"Above you. Grandmother or aunt?"

"An aunt."

Quickly, Dave's dad got back in. He gave me the feeling that he was somehow well-known, that he had some sort of presence in the world. "He's telling me he was written about when he passed."

"That's true," Dave said.

"Twice, actually. He's telling me two things were written about him."

"Yes."

"He's not telling me in a cocky way. But this was a big thing for him. Who had the impact to the body? He's talking about this impact."

"My father."

"Okay, was he shot? Because he's giving me the feeling of an impact. But it doesn't feel all-encompassing. It feels like in one area. Now have you done something recently on a computer for your dad? Or do you have something on your computer connected to your dad? What's the connection? He's showing me doing something on a computer."

"Oh, I did write something. His eulogy."

"Is it still on your computer?"

"I think so."

"Who's the 'P'? He's acknowledging a 'P-A'."

"My wife, possibly. Pat."

"Is she the accountant or you?"

"I am."

"Okay, then around your wife there's something about health care. I see white all around her. White to me is health care. And I see her with a very holistic and spiritual approach. Either she's into homeopathic medicine . . ."

"You're right about that. She's a chiropractor, very into a holistic approach."

At this point Dave's father started to do something very unusual and exciting. Instead of a series of single images—the usual way I get visual information—it was as if he was turning my mind into a movie camera. He began taking me on a little tour, a trip along a main street in a downtown area near where I lived. I told Dave that his father was first showing me a particular bookstore, not one of the big chains but a popular independent book store called Book Revue. I assume he did this to establish where we were starting from. Now he took me across the street to another store I knew, a gift gallery. "Now he's taking me up the street," I told Dave. "I'm being shown a Burger King."

Dave laughed, as if both amused and amazed.

"Why's your dad taking me over there?" I asked.

"My office is right there," he said. "Right across from the Burger King."

I pounded the desk. I loved his father's enterprise. "I'm sitting here and thinking, 'Why's he showing me the Book Revue and why's he showing me Burger King?' And I was going to ask you, 'Did you go buy a book and have lunch at Burger King before you came here? I didn't know if I was supposed to be talking about a bookstore and fast food."

"It's like he led you by the hand, down the street right to the front door of my office."

"That's his way of showing it's him and he's okay. He's telling me to tell you that he's okay on the Other Side. Now, the only reason he can do that is he knows I know that street. But I just feel like there are a lot of things connected . . . I'm getting a feeling like sandpaper, an abrasive feeling. I don't get this as being a smooth, always easy-going kind of relationship from what he's showing me. . . . What does August mean? What's the symbolic nature of August?"

"Birthday," Dave said.

"Yours?"

"My mother's."

"Okay. That's your dad's way of acknowledging your mother. He's taking me to the month of August and he's saying it has two meanings, not one. It must be two birthdays."

"No, one, but her birthday is eight-eight. August eighth."

"That's what he shows me, he shows me eight twice, eight-eight. Has mom remarried, or is she dating?"

"No."

"Is she going out more?"

"She's doing things."

"He's showing me her starting a new life or a lot of new things around her. He sees her differently now, and it's not that now that he's made a transition he sees her differently. I think he's trying to show me that she's different. This is not about a physical move, it's about her as a person."

"Maybe I should disclose to you how he passed on," Dave said.

"Was he killed?" I asked.

"Yes."

"I know that, because he was acknowledging to me that he was killed, and that there was an impact, something that affected his body, like he was hit in the head. I feel like it's one blunt thing that does this, that takes him out. But he's showing me a change of perception on life that your mother now has."

"True."

"Now, was he hit in the head?"

"Yes."

"He shows me he gets hit in the head and he goes out. He might have passed later, but he's showing me that he goes out there. Now, his physical body was sustained for a while?"

"Yes."

"Was that four hours later or four days later? Or am I in the month of April, the fourth month?"

"Yeah, you're in April. He died in April."

"He's showing me four. But he wants you to know that he's okay on the Other Side. Was someone else with him? Or somebody was supposed to go with him and didn't go? There's a feeling of shoulda-coulda-woulda been there with him. . . . He's giving me the feeling that . . . I want to say it's your mom.

"Now, does he have a brother that's passed?"

"Yes."

"He's telling me that he's with his brother. His brother passed before him, like a year and a half to two years before him?"

"Yes, about that time period."

"Was there a house for sale about that time or something with real estate? He's showing me the selling of a house, the moving of a house. Is somebody selling a house now? Either I'm supposed to be saying that the brother has some connection to real estate, the selling of a house, or that someone around you is selling a house."

"Oh, that is true. My brother is thinking about selling his house."

"I don't think that's it. Who's the Rick or Rich?"

"Rich. A close friend of my father's."

"Is he still here? Still alive?"

"Yes. In fact, that's the house. He's selling his house and I'm doing the closing tomorrow morning."

"He's got to watch his health."

"Yes, he has cancer."

"Do you have any connection to Egypt? Are you going there, have you been there? I'm watching myself draw these pyramids. There's a connection here somewhere. It's coming from one of the people that we're talking to. And I've been doing this since we first started. I just realized what I was doing."

"Rich's wife went to Egypt."

At this point, I felt Dave's father's energy beginning to step back. I could sense that Dave had some unsettled feelings about his father's death and I wanted to see if he had any questions while his presence was still fairly strong. "Anything you want to ask him that I can try to get him to answer for you?"

Dave had indeed come with questions. As I later learned, his father had died just four months before, and the wound was fresh. It was not an ordinary death; in fact, it took seven agonizing years from start to finish. It started one awful twilight in February of 1989. Dave's father, seventy years old and still working as a pharmacist in Brooklyn, was attacked during a robbery by a masked man who took the money, then visciously pistol-whipped his victim on the head. Dave's father managed to make his way out to the street, intending to drive home. Then, he collapsed. It was, in a real sense, the end of his life. For the next seven years, he lived in a state that alternated between semiconscious and virtually comatose. He was in two hospitals and a rehabilitation center in Pennsylvania before being brought to the place he would live the last six years of his life, a nursing home not far from where his eldest son lived. There, Dave and his mother would visit Sunday after Sunday, month after month, year after year.

In the early years, there were times when Dave might see a faint smile or nod from his father, a sign of some cognition; but most times, the old man was just not there. In the first year or two, Dave and his mother hoped for signs of improvement. But in the last years, they had to face the reality that he was gone, mentally if not yet physically. He had been murdered, but the final, inevitable passage was being kept on indefinite hold for reasons only God knew. Death finally came in the spring of 1996. As Dave's father had told me with a sense of pride and pleasure during the reading, his death was noted twice in the newspaper. Besides an obituary, there was a poignant article by a local newspaper columnist, a friend of Dave's who wrote not only about what a decent, gentle, and hardworking man Dave's father was—in his 70s, still working as a druggist in a tough neighborhood far from his suburban home—but also about the tragic circumstances of his long, hard death and what it was like for his family.

"There was so much to tell him, and so they tried to keep him abreast," the columnist wrote of Dave's father. "The marriage of his younger son, and the marriage of his older son, and the thousand family details in between . . . These family events were relayed in one-sided conversations that would last for as long as the teller could maintain the energy it took. And for all anyone knew, he was happy to hear of them, though in the last seven years of his life it was impossible to know what communication passed between him and the rest of the world. He could open his eyes. He could put his feet on the floor at the edge of his bed. Until his health began its final decline, he could use one hand to push himself a short way in his wheelchair."

"Did he know that I was visiting him?" Dave asked me now. That was his biggest question. "Did he know I was there for him?"

I got a positive feeling. His father definitely knew. And the question from his son seemed to momentarily reinvigorate him. His energy came back strongly.

"Was there any consciousness on his part?" Dave asked.

"Spiritually there was consciousness. Physically, there was none. I don't see him being very responsive on a physical level. On a spiritual level, when they're in a coma, they're definitely there. . . . He probably had an easy transition because of how long he was in a coma." But of course, it was also a very long transition, one that was painful for his family—accounting for the "here and there, in-your-life-out-of-your-life" feeling his father had given me at the beginning of the reading. That's also why I had gotten that emotionally distant, sandpaperlike feel about their relationship. It didn't mean they had a bad relationship, as those feelings often indicate. In this case, it meant that his father's condition obviously made for an extremely difficult relationship for both sides.

Suddenly, I had the sensation of giving something physically, out of the body. "Were you going to donate blood for him?" I asked Dave.

"No."

"What was donated? Did Dad donate his organs?"

"No."

"He's talking about the donation of something. Not money. Physically."

Dave didn't relate to that information, which was perplexing to me because it was coming through strongly. He asked me if I was getting anything about the baby he and his wife were planning to adopt. "I feel like there are delays attached to it," I said. "But don't get discouraged. Your dad is giving me the feeling of telling you to be excited about this. It's a positive thing. Now he's showing me a model boat with sails, like those boats that are in bottles? Is this anything that you have that was his? Is he trying to tell me about sailing? He's stepping back. When they step back like that, that's their way of breaking their energy with me. But he is showing me what looks like an old pirate boat. Also, are you putting in a pool? Because he wants me to acknowledge spending time around a pool. Sometimes, they like to come through with information you don't understand, and you'll leave here and two weeks from now you'll come in contact with this thing, and that's your dad's way of saying, 'See, I *was* there.' "

I later heard that Dave and his wife were joining a yacht club, mostly for its main feature: a large pool. These details, among the others I had given him, validated for Dave his father's presence. And it provided a measure of comfort for him, knowing that his father was aware of his many visits through those painful years. It was what had nagged at him throughout the ordeal, and continued after the funeral. Now he knew that his weekly visits and family updates were not in vain. He was making the most important connection of all: a spiritual one.

As Dave left, he crossed paths with my next appointment, a dark-haired woman in her early thirties named Dina Grgas. A friendly and upbeat woman, she sat erect, anxious to get started.

"Have you ever been read by a psychic or a medium?" I asked.

"Well, once when I went to the Feast of San Genaro in Little Italy," Dina said. "She tried to get me to buy all these crystals."

"And I'll bet she put a curse on you," I said with a laugh.

I then explained what was going to happen. "Your job," I said, "is to verify and confirm what I'm being told by giving me a yes or no—that's it. You don't want to add to it, you don't want to give me any information that's going to be leading."

She nodded and handed me her watch. I held it, closed my eyes, and after a few seconds of concentration, I felt the presence of a woman above her who had crossed to the Other Side.

"It's my grandmother," she said.

"Hold on. We'll see who it is. Was your grandmother on your mom's side?"

"Yes."

"Did your grandfather pass over?"

"Yes."

"Because she's acknowledging that her mate is with her. Now, who looks like her?"

"My mother does."

"She's talking about a parallel between her and someone beneath her. She looks *a lot* like her. Is your mom starting to say, 'My God, I'm looking just like my mother'—that kind of thing?"

"Exactly."

"Especially around the eyes, your grandmother is saying."

"That's true."

"Who had the diabetes?"

"She did."

"Now, do you have relatives living out of New York?"

"Oh yeah, plenty."

"Any living south of New York, like North Carolina, South Carolina, or going down toward Florida, but not quite there? Someone's pulling me to that area. Do you have anybody there?"

"I don't think so."

"Yes, you do." Despite what Dina was saying, someone was focusing my attention very strongly on that part of the country. This was to be the turning point in the reading. What followed was a fascinating trail to a very unusual source. It was a fairly long and winding road, but an illuminating one, so rather than edit it down to the essentials, I will present it fully.

I began hearing a "D" name—possibly David or Daniel—who was being acknowledged by someone above Dina. But this wasn't connecting with her. Neither did a male with blackness in the lungs, indicating lung cancer or possibly emphysema or tuberculosis. "I'm outside New York State," I reminded her, a bit frustrated. "Your dad's family must come from out of state."

"My parents are originally from what was formerly Yugoslavia. And they also have quite a bit of family in Canada and California."

"No, I'm definitely being taken down the East Coast."

"Is it a male?" Dina asked, her tone suggesting she had suddenly remembered someone.

I couldn't tell yet. All I knew was that it was someone connected to her who was south of New York but above Florida. I concentrated and told Dina I was asking her grandmother for some help. "She seems like a strong woman."

"Very."

"Because I'm getting a very strong impression. I'm asking her to sort of take care of people over there, like get them in line and make them come through a little easier so I understand who's trying to come through." As I talked, I got a strong feeling—again, down the East Coast, but now I felt I was being actively pulled. I grabbed a sheet of notepaper and quickly jotted a rough map of the east coast of the United States. "Don't laugh at my map. I was never great at geography. But here we are in New York, and I am being pulled straight down." Again it was like Paul's father guiding me down the street to his law office. Only this time someone was guiding me through states, by feel rather than by sight. "I'm below New Jersey," I said, drawing a line with my pen to show where I was being led. "Now I'm below Pennsylvania, I'm below Delaware and below— what's next, Maryland? I'm between Maryland and Georgia. You have ties here. Who is between Maryland and Georgia?"

"Is Virginia there?" Dina asked, apparently even worse at geography than me but apparently thinking of someone from there.

"Is there someone who's crossed over who's from there? Because someone is insisting that I come down to this area. Is there someone who's passed on that lived in this area? Or are you going there?"

"I do plan on it."

"Okay, because I'm being told there's a connection. Is this someone that you were involved with, that you were dating, or someone you were just good friends with?"

"None of the above," Dina said, chuckling. Now it was clear I was zeroing in on someone. Was this the person she came for?

"None of the above? Well, he's putting himself to your side—husband, brother, cousin, friend. Is this a male?"

"Yes. It's hard to describe the relationship. It's not a blood relation."

"I can only go with what I'm shown. It's not above you, not below you, he's putting himself to your side. And that he's connected in this area of the country. Did he pass near an historic site?"

"That I don't know."

"Is he by Williamsburg? Or Virginia Beach?"

"Down in Virginia. I don't know where."

I stared past Dina, trying hard to get more. "What's the 'Da' connection there? I'm hearing a 'Da' sounding name, like Daniel or David or . . . I'll settle for the D, because I'm hearing the dominant sound of the 'D'."

"His father's name is Doug."

"He's acknowledging the 'D'. That's the first thing. Are Mom and Dad split?"

"His adoptive parents are together."

"He's telling me parents, and he splits his parents."

"His birth parents maybe. Or he may be trying to indicate two separate sets of parents."

"Now, is he slightly younger than you?"

"Yes."

"Because he's putting himself as being younger than you. But he's showing himself as being like a friend to you. He's insisting I put him to your side but now he's telling me he's younger than you."

"Yes."

"Was there a lack of communication, or did you not get a chance to speak with him? Did you guys write back and forth to each other? He's showing me writing."

"I write to his mom. I keep in touch with his mom. In fact, I mailed a letter to her today."

"He's talking about writing back and forth. Now he says that you're *affiliated* with him. Like you did something for him. Okay, or you're connected with him on the periphery, on the fringe. You didn't meet him. He's telling me now you didn't know him. Like you know *about* him, but you don't know him."

"That's exactly right."

"Did you ever question whether you did the right thing or worry about what would be appropriate? He's telling me that you did the right thing. That whatever was done, there was an appropriateness to it."

"I guess, in my own mind, I worried."

"Hold on. Was there a drug problem around him? Somebody who did something with drugs? Or was he on very heavy medication? He's showing me a symbol for heavy toxins in the body or drugs, or medicine. Who's Rick, or Richard, or Robert?"

"A doctor that I know."

"But it's connected to him. I'm hearing 'R'. Was he a kid? Because he's making me say he's a kid. Now, was he killed, or did his actions lead to his passing? Because he's giving me the feeling of a violence to his passing. Is that correct?"

"Yes."

"He wants his mom to know he came through and he's okay. He also wants this 'R' to know—Robbie or Richie, sounds like Rick."

Dina sighed heavily. "Rick," she confirmed, sticking to my instruction not to volunteer information.

"He's showing me water, like this happened by the water. I also feel like I'm down. All of a sudden, he's making me feel like I'm going down. This wasn't a plane crash, correct?"

"No."

"I feel like I'm going down, but I'm outside. And I don't feel like I'm suffering from a fall. It's like a controllable . . . was this a vehicle accident, did he go off the side of the road?"

"It was a vehicle accident. I don't know the details."

"It had to go down, go over an embankment . . . I feel like I'm going down. And I do feel like he passed very quickly. Now, I just need to know how you're affiliated with him. Because he's making a big deal out of this. Like your relationship is the thing. He's showing me him being a balloon and you holding the string. Like he's out there and you're just standing there holding this. Like you're not even a family friend. He's telling me he does not know you, he's never met you."

"Which is all true."

"That you're not connected to him, that you were brought into . . . almost like you spoke about him. He's trying to say that you spoke about it or you did something about him. You know what I'm saying? He's showing me symbolism of doing something for the person without meeting them. I think he's saying you did something for him. I guess it could go either way. He did something for you."

"He did much more for me than I did for him."

"Who's Jim? Or a 'J' and an 'M' or an 'N'. He's rattling off a whole bunch of names to me. He's acknowledging Jim, two 'J's connected to him. I think one's a Jim and maybe a John, two short 'J' names. . . . Was he in the hospital? Did you see him in the hospital? Why is he putting you in the hospital? Were you in the hospital?"

"Yes."

"He's telling me there's a connection between you and him in the hospital."

"Yes."

"Did you get an organ from him?"

Dina smiled and nodded in a way that told me that this was why she had come. "That's it," she said. "I had a liver transplant. This boy, Chuck, was my donor."

"That's the donation!" I exclaimed. I went right past how wonderful it was that Dina's liver donor—a person she never knew but who had saved her life—had come through, and seized instead on a loose end of the previous reading. It shows you how preoccupied I can become by the nuts and bolts of my work. Dina, of course, had no idea what I was talking about. "I had someone right before you," I explained. "The guy who was leaving when you got here. His father came through, and he was telling me he donated something—blood, an organ. At least I thought it was him. But it was this kid. That's why he didn't repeat it, he didn't tell me again specifically that he donated an organ, because he had told me before. That tells you how they talk to you. You were downstairs. You came with this kid and I was picking it up."

This was not the first time something like this had happened. I told Dina about one of my favorite experiences. It involved a man who came to my office with his wife and daughter-in-law but had no intention of being read himself. He was a nonbeliever, very stoic about the whole thing. His daughter-in-law came upstairs first and sat down. I started giving her all kinds of information but none of it made sense to her. It was a truly terrible reading, and I was embarrassed. Finally, I said, "I have to apologize to you. I might not be the person to read you. Let me try one more time." I said to the spirits, "Listen, be a little more specific, please. This lady's got no clue." And they said to me: "Ski." I turned to the woman and asked, "Do you ski?" She said no. But they were definitely telling me to say "Ski." Did it mean a last name that ended with "ski?" The woman thought a moment, then said, "Wait a minute. That's what they used to call my father-in-law." I got up, left the room, leaned over the railing, and called down to him: "Excuse me, did they use to call you 'Ski'?" Yes, the man said, a bit nervously. "And did your father pass?" Yes. "Would you please come upstairs?" I spent the entire session talking to him about his dad and his relatives. He identified with everything that meant nothing to his daughter-in-law.

That's what happened with Dina. When I later reviewed the tape, I discovered the actual timing of this spiritual mix-up: on the tape, the doorbell is heard ringing just a few minutes after the organ donation message had come through toward the end of Paul's reading.

So Dina—and the spirit of her liver donor who came with her—were in the neighborhood.

"I kept insisting it was his father," I explained to Dina. "I didn't know it was another person, your donor. He had to show me both of you in the hospital to let me know what was going on. And I knew at that moment that he had been here earlier."

Knowing the outcome, if you go back a few pages and reread the transcript of this session, you can get a fuller appreciation of how this works. You can track how Chuck's spirit directed me right to the Virginia area—of all places in the world—and then kept me focused on his unusual relationship with Dina, describing what it wasn't to get me to understand what it was. Normally if there's a vagueness about whether a spirit was a brother or a cousin, it doesn't bog me down. We just move on. But because this was such a unique relationship, *that* became the message—the validation. Most interesting—even poetic—was the image he used to convey how they were connected. He was a balloon, way up in the air, and she was holding the string. And then, finally, he showed me the two of them in the hospital together. Dina told me that the "Rick" that Chuck was acknowledging was indeed an important person connected to both of them: he was her transplant surgeon.

Chuck helped Dina tremendously by just showing up, of course. She felt she owed him so much. From birth until age twenty-five, she had suffered from an extremely rare, genetic liver disorder called Crigler-Najjar disease. It was so deadly that Dina, though she had some close calls, was one of the relative few who had managed to live past childhood. But to survive this particular variety of liver malfunction, Dina had to be constantly exposed to light. Among other things, it meant she had to sleep unclothed and under special lamps, though even then her skin had the yellow cast of jaundice. That all changed when she received the liver of a Virginia teenager who slid off the road in a fatal one-vehicle accident in 1990. Dina was twenty-five when she wore pajamas and slept in the dark for the first time. When she came to me six years later, at thirty-one, she was the oldest survivor of the disease in the world. She looked perfectly normal and healthy, with no hint of what she'd been through—on the outside.

Dina felt so connected to Chuck, and yet he remained strangely unknown to her. She had yearned to thank him, and she felt he displayed his openness to this overture, even his love, by coming through as she had hoped. He gave her an even more explicit message of comfort when he addressed Dina's worries about whether she had done "the right thing." This concerned her decision to contact his parents. When she received Chuck's liver six years before, she wanted to write to them to express her gratitude and her sympathy. But she felt somewhat awkward about it. She eventually decided to write to them, and she and Chuck's mother had since struck up an active friendship through letters and phone calls. Dina was even planning a trip to Virginia to meet Chuck's family for the first time. Through me, Chuck told her that was a good thing.

"I hope he knows how much I appreciate what he did for me," Dina said. "That's why I keep in touch with his mother. That's why I came."

"Oh, he knows," I assured her.

I later learned that just a few days before his accident, Chuck had been watching a television show that talked about organ donation. He turned to his sister and said, "I want to do that." His sister was shocked. It didn't seem like something Chuck would be concerned about.

"I'm getting someone with a 'Ra' sounding name," I told Dina. Chuck had stepped back and was letting another spirit come through.

"My sister?" Dina wondered.

"Sounds like maybe Rachel," I said.

"It's Croation. Radoicha."

"I wouldn't have gotten that. She's on the Other Side?"

"Yeah."

"She's been there quite a while?"

"Oh, a long time."

"Because this kid—your donor—is acknowledging that 'R' is here and that this person has been there for quite a while. Did she have a blood disorder, or a problem with her blood? Or her spleen?"

"No."

"You're sure? She didn't have a white blood cell problem or a major infection in her body?"

"There was a problem, but it wasn't in her blood."

"Had to. Had to have affected her blood. Had to. This I'll stand by. Because she's specifically showing me something that affects her entire body and it goes through the blood. How old was your sister?"

"Seven months old."

"Something affected her blood. I'm telling you, there was something wrong with her blood. What did they say she passed from? SIDS?"

"No. It's a rare liver disease. Very, very rare, but genetic. Which is why I needed a liver."

"Tell me exactly what happened. If I'm not familiar with this liver disease, they're going to give it to me the best way they can, the blood. What happens to the liver?"

"Well, my liver and my sister's liver didn't produce certain enzymes that are supposed to break down bilirubin."

"Which would be in your blood."

"Right."

"Thank you. Your sister is around you and your young friend is the one who's bringing her through, letting me know that she's here also. It's a way of showing that we're all connected on the Other Side."

DELIVERING THE GOODS

Sometimes mediums are accused of being "just mind readers." I've heard this from skeptics myself. They theorize that we are picking up brain waves from our clients and misattributing them to the "spirits" of dead people. As one version of this theory goes, it doesn't have to be what's on people's minds at the moment. Anything in the recesses of the brain—anything a person has ever known, even subconsciously—is supposedly accessible to us. Of course, such skeptics find this an impressive feat, just not quite as impressive as talking to the dead.

In the years that I have been doing this work, I have had only one moment when I thought the skeptics might be right. It happened in the early years, when I was in college and still developing as a medium. I was conducting a group reading at a psychic seminar. I sat before about eighteen people arranged in a semicircle, with a room of people watching from the background. I gave the group my standard caveats: the

19

spirits we hope to hear from don't always come through, and if they do they don't always give us what we want to hear. I instructed them to listen carefully, but not to stretch something to make it fit.

Midway through the session, I made a strong connection with a young lady's mother. She was full of energy and came through for nearly twenty minutes with so much specific, detailed information that it was like a running water faucet. I related to the situation because the young lady was about my age, and my own mother had passed fairly recently. The mother's spirit gave me everything but the most common information: the manner of her passing, and when it happened. I tried to elicit this from her, but for some reason she didn't answer. Finally, she began to step back—a feeling of retreat I get when a spirit can't sustain the level of energy needed to communicate—and when I couldn't feel the information coming through strongly any longer, I looked at her daughter and saw that her face was filled with relief, peace, and emotional closure. But I was curious about one thing. "What did your mother die from?" I asked. "And when did she pass? Your mom wouldn't tell me."

"That's because she didn't," she said. "She's not dead."

I was shocked and instantly overwhelmed by a thought that paralyzed me with doubt: *Oh my God—I am a mind reader. I'm not talking to a dead person, and I never have.* These thoughts rushed through my head, and I could feel myself getting hotter and hotter. Then I quickly got a grip on the moment, and said, "Wait a minute. What do you mean your mother didn't pass?" The young woman explained that her mother was in a coma, and had been for several years. I realized she was coming through as though she *had* crossed over; perhaps because she was on the precipice, straddling two worlds.

And I was relieved to reassure myself that I was not "just a mind reader."

It's easy, I suppose, for me to say I simply know what it is I'm doing and not doing. But while *I* know the information is coming from the Other Side, I must admit that I relish instances that give me a chance to prove it. The story of Dina in the previous chapter is one such example. Chuck, her liver donor, gave me several pieces of information that Dina could not confirm. She didn't know, for example, the details of Chuck's accident. When I said I was getting a feeling of being pulled down, I believed Chuck was telling me that he went off a road and down an embankment. Dina said she didn't know anything about his accident. But later, I found out from Chuck's mother that this was just what had happened. She also said I was right when I said that the accident occurred near the historical area of Williamsburg, Virginia.

There aren't too many professions in which a practitioner is required to start from scratch virtually every day—to prove not only his ability, but his *legitimacy*, all over again, every time out. Of course, given the intangible, cosmic nature of my work, it's not surprising that I must constantly deliver the goods to prove that I'm doing what I say I'm doing. Though most people who come to me for readings believe in what I do (or at least believe it's possible) hardly a day goes by that I don't have to prove it to someone new, whether it's a confirmed cynic or a fence-sitter, someone who's just not sure what he or she believes.

I was twenty-six when I decided to leave my hospital job to do this work full-time. Although I knew it was the right thing to do, it was not an easy decision. For one thing, I was giving up the security of my job, and I don't mean this in the financial sense only. I had spent years in school getting my degree in public health and administration, and I had worked hard to attain a position of responsibility. I was in charge of training eight hundred nurses on the hospital computer system, and was rising within the ranks of the hospital's administration. My psychic work remained in the background. I was a professional, and I was proud to tell people what I did for a living. But now, when someone asked what I did, I had to get used to saying, "I'm a psychic medium." There was no getting around the fact that it was not a widely respected field. I'm sure that what comes to mind for many people are images of gypsies, fortune-tellers, storefront "psychics." Con artists taking people's money. Of course, the discomfort that comes with being associated with such a rogues' gallery is balanced by the knowledge that I am helping people in a way that's impossible to put a value on.

"Performing" for the media is always an interesting and challenging proposition. Whether it is on television, radio or in print, high-profile psychics are always under pressure to give not only good readings, but great ones. I accept and understand that, though I also accept the fact that I have little to do with whether a reading is good, great, mediocre, or bad. At this stage, my ability is more or less constant. What changes is who's coming through, how clearly, and how well the recipient is tuned in. Yes, there are ways to increase the chances of a good reading—positive, meditative energies on both sides being at the top of the list—but there are, of course, no guarantees. The irony is that once a medium gets a good reputation, he or she will be held to a high standard, but with no control over whether a particular reading will meet that standard.

I would be lying if I said it wasn't sometimes frustrating to feel as though I am being asked to jump through hoops, especially since I have so little control over the result. However, I see it as a critical part of my job to reach as many people as possible. I want everyone to know there is more after this life. I want them to know that if spirits are coming through they are coming through for a reason. And just as important, I want them to know that this is not a 1-900-PSYCHIC line, that their relatives and friends *are* around them and they're okay, but that this is not some "Dial-the-Dead" service. This book is one way I hope to open the lines of communication with the Other Side. Appearing in the media is another. So when a reporter or producer wants proof, I want to accommodate. But it doesn't always mean the results are what I hope they'll be.

It's reality that the world is made up of people who believe and disbelieve all kinds of things, based on their own personal experiences, intellectual processes, religious backgrounds, and other factors. Some people have faith in the afterlife; it's just what they believe, and probably believed all their lives. Some are confirmed nonbelievers.

There's nothing I or any other medium can do to convince them. And in the middle—maybe the largest group—are people who are open to the possibilities. All they need is a personal experience to grasp. Like the general population, the media world contains people in all these groups.

I once got a phone call from a producer from one of the more popular daytime talk shows, who had heard me on the morning show of WPLJ in New York, which I appear on regularly. "We'd really like to have you on," the TV producer said, "but I'd like you to do a reading for me first."

"Sure," I said.

"Go ahead," she said.

"Right now, on the phone?" I asked. I had assumed she meant she wanted me to arrange a reading. Though I have done many readings on the phone (including many for callers to radio and television programs), I prepare for them with a regular series of meditation and visualization exercises, just as I prepare for every reading I do. But I felt that this producer was basically saying: Read me right now, and if you don't give me something that will knock my socks off, it means everything I heard you do on the radio is a setup and a hoax and you're a fraud.

When I told her this is what I felt that she was saying, she said, no, no. "All I'm saying is that if I have my own experience, I can go back to my boss and say, 'Hey, this guy is legitimate.' " I told her I really wasn't in a reading mode, and that I'd be happy to set something up for later, but the woman was relentless; that's what people in her job do every day, I guess. Because I feel that I am a member of a "helping" profession, and because I do want my message to get out, my instinct is to say yes in situations like these, even against my better judgment. I gave in and read her. When I was done, she said the information was vague and not really connected to her. I never heard from her again.

In the few years since I decided to devote all of my professional energies to mediumship, I've gotten a steady flow of calls from radio stations around the country wanting me to do readings on the air. In most cases, the hosts are helpful and positive, but occasionally I'll get a Howard Stern wannabe who's just looking for a foil.

I have a policy of not reading hosts on the air, whether it's radio or television. The reason is that when I do a reading, I need the person to really tune in to what we're doing. Someone who's the host of a radio show has too many things on his mind. It takes too much energy to be charismatic and entertaining enough to carry a show, leaving nothing left to focus on what I'm saying. I will read other people in the studio, and I'll do callers. But I'll only read the host off the air.

I once agreed to go on a show in Toledo and the host said, "I want you to read me." We were on the air.

"No," I said.

"No?" he replied. "You don't get it. You're on my show. When they give you your own show, you can do whatever you want."

I explained my policy. "Benny, I'll read you off the air," I said. "I'll read you on a commercial break. I will read you tomorrow. But I am not reading you live on the show."

There was dead air. Then, the host said, "Well, what do you want to do? Do you want to take calls?"

"Sure," I said. "I'd love to do that." And I read several people on the phone and eventually won the host over. But the bottom line is that I can't worry about what everyone thinks. If I did, every time I gave a lecture to three hundred people, I would think, "How am I doing? Am I convincing them?" I would have to call three hundred people afterward and ask, "Was I good? Are you a believer?"

*I*t was a perfect summer Sunday in 1993 and Sally and Anthony DiSabato were having friends and family over, the plans no more complicated than food and fun in the backyard, everyone lounging around the pool, kids splish-splashing the hours away.

The DiSabatos were inside putting the food together when a pitcher of iced tea dropped to the floor as Sally was taking it out of the refrigerator. She spent the next few minutes cleaning up the mess, making sure to find every little sliver of broken glass so her children, nine-year-old Cara and three-and-a-half-year-old Michael, wouldn't cut their bare feet.

Sally was finishing up when her mother-in-law came in and asked, "Where's Mikey?"

Sally looked around. Mikey had been in the house at one point while she was cleaning up the broken glass, but she hadn't noticed where he went after that. She went upstairs to his room. "Mikey," she called out. No Mikey. "And the next gut feeling I had," she recalls, "was, 'Go to the pool.' "

She went downstairs and out through the sliding glass door that led from the house to the deck. The pool was just a few steps away, and when she got there, Sally felt any parent's worst nightmare come full force. Her child was floating facedown in the pool. She screamed out, startling the preoccupied group sitting at a table near the pool. Hearing Sally, Anthony came out, jumped into the pool, pulled Mikey out, and began CPR. Mikey was rushed to the hospital and placed on life support.

"He had to walk by everybody who was sitting at the table," Sally remembers. "I was inside cleaning up the iced tea. He must have gone back through the doors and just walked past everybody at the table. And just went in the pool. And that was it. He was very quiet, nobody heard a thing. He just kind of snuck past everyone. And what was just so amazing about the whole thing was that Michael never did anything in a quiet way."

Mikey was disconnected from life support a few days later.

Six months later

"Did you lose a child recently?" I asked a woman named Donna Kaplowitz, early in her reading.

"No," she said.

"Did someone in your family lose a child?"

"Yes," she said.

"Are you the child's godmother?"

"No."

"But you were very close with this child, you always watched over him."

"Yes."

"Is he your nephew?"

"Yes."

"He wants you to know he's okay. . . . Do you know a Michael, or a Mark?"

"Yes, Michael."

"He's your nephew?"

"Yes."

"I feel like it's hard to breathe." I put my hands on my chest. "My body also feels like it's being shocked. I see blood. Is your nephew passing due to health reasons?"

"No."

"I'll keep asking him." I chuckled and told Donna, "I don't mean to laugh but I keep asking your nephew what the main cause was and he just told me, 'No!' "

Donna smiled. "That's Michael," she said. "When it's no, it's no."

Now Michael told me he was around for a few days. "He was in a coma," I said. "There was a big decision that had to be made. Was this decision to take him off life support?"

"Yes."

"He wants you to go back and tell his father that he understands. It was like he was banging his head against the wall to make this decision. It's important that you go back and tell him he understands."

"I will," Donna said.

"Who is Anna or Anthony? Oh, he just told me, that's his dad."

"Yes!"

Now Michael began running down a list of people who were taking care of him on the Other Side, including his great-grandmother, whose name was Mary, and a priest who had recently crossed over. "Do you know someone, a family friend, who's a priest that has recently passed on?" I asked.

"Yes!" Donna said excitedly. ("I almost fell off the couch at that," Donna said later. "Anthony's parents were very close to a priest, who had married Sally and Anthony and married my brother and sister-in-law. And he had passed on three months before.")

"He's one of the people taking care of Michael. This is very important. You must go back and tell his mother that he is being well taken care of. She feels that he's all alone, but he's not. He wants you to go back and tell her he's in good hands."

Donna promised she would.

Now Michael acknowledged a friend he played with. "Lisa or Laurie."

"I know a Lori," Donna said, thinking Michael was acknowledging a friend of hers, a nurse who had flown up from Florida and spent a lot of time with Michael while he was on life support.

"No," I said. "The friend he plays with."

Donna thought a moment. "Oh, *Laura*. She lives right across the street. She was his buddy, they played together all the time."

Now Michael began talking about a wedding. He said he was dressed like the groom. "Was he in a tux?" I asked.

"Yes."

"Because he says that's what you told him to get him to wear it, that the groom was wearing the same thing." Now he told me that he was standing by the band, doing something cute.

(Donna didn't understand this. But she later learned from a relative that during the cocktail hour, while she was outside taking pictures, Michael had played onstage, dancing and singing as the band played "Achy Breaky Heart.")

I asked Donna about the sneakers her nephew kept showing me. "What's with these sneakers?" I asked. "Was he buried in sneakers? But he's making me feel like these were the 'wrong' sneakers."

"He was buried in sneakers," Donna confirmed. "But not his favorite sneakers."

"Okay, now he says this is for you: He's telling me about a one-piece jumpsuit, or pajamas, with a picture on the front. He says you'll understand this."

"Yes," she said quietly, without elaborating. (Donna later said that she had taken care of Michael the morning that he drowned, while his parents were out food shopping. He was wearing one-piece "feety" pajamas with the Superman emblem on the front.) He also showed me a Winnie-the-Pooh bear. Donna said that Michael's mother and another aunt called him "Pooh."

Now Michael switched gears, acknowledging the pain his passing had caused his family. He wanted his grandmother to know he was all right. But most of all, he wanted that message to get through to his mother. "This is very important," I told Donna. "Go back and tell your sister that when she thinks Michael is around, it's not because she wishes he was, but that he *is* there. Tell her it's important."

Donna didn't need me to tell her how important it was. She knew how much her sister needed to hear exactly that. Sally DiSabato had always believed in heaven, but now it made her upset. "I was worried as a mother," she explains. "Michael was only three-and-a-half. He was still a baby. So I had this terrible feeling: Where is he? Who's taking care of him? I'm supposed to be taking care of him. I don't know where he is."

Michael's father, meanwhile, had no belief in an afterlife: "Pretty much when you're dead, you're dead." His grief was focused on the here and now.

Sally and Anthony were in Lake Tahoe when Donna called and told them about her reading with me. It was a place with bittersweet memories: The family owned a timeshare in Tahoe, and their previous trip was the only time they had been to the resort with Michael. He had loved playing in the snow there and talked about it until the day he died. So he was on their minds a lot when Sally's sister, still on a high from the reading, called with the incredible news that she had just heard from Michael.

Sally was stunned. "I was just like, Whoa!" she remembers. "Especially the part about him wanting me to know that he really was around me. Because it just confirmed everything that had been going on, that it was Mikey."

What had been going on, Sally recounts, was a string of strange incidents that occurred in the months after her son's death. "First was the door rattling upstairs. It was late one night, maybe two or three months after the accident. It was a pocket door between our bedroom and bathroom and it never rattled. And I said, 'Hi, Mikey.' Then, a couple of months after that, in the winter, I was talking to my uncle in the kitchen one day and we were talking about Michael when all of a sudden, a couple of leaves on a plant that was sitting on the counter started to bob up and down. Out of nowhere. And I said, 'See, Joe, he knows we're talking about him.'

"A short time after that, we got the first snow. It was a very sentimental day, because of our memories of Mikey at Lake Tahoe. I went outside and wrote in the snow, 'Hi Mikey.' Later that night, we had just come home from a movie when the light in the exercise room went on by itself, and I knew it was him. For the longest time, Anthony would say to me, 'But Sal, I never get these signs.' I told him, 'They're there, you just miss them.' One time when we were having this conversation, we were in the car, coming home from somewhere, when he felt like somebody kicked his seat from the back. It was a loud thump. I heard it too. We were alone in the car and there was nothing in the back seat. I know because I looked. And just then, on the radio at that moment—Anthony had just changed the station—was Garth Brooks singing "The Dance." That song always reminded Anthony of Mikey, and we played it at his funeral. I said, 'You see, there he is, clear as day.'

"Then, when we were in Lake Tahoe—the night before Donna went for her reading back in New York—I woke out of my sleep yelling, 'Michael, Michael,' and I felt this brush on my cheek. The next day, Donna called and told us about the reading and gave me that message that he wanted me to know that it really was him all those times. It just confirmed everything that I knew in my heart."

I saved this story for last because it has a special meaning for me. I don't know why, but the spirit of Michael DiSabato has become as close to me as any I have encountered through my work. He is in a select group that includes Andrew Miracolo, the boy who came to me on my honeymoon, and Tracy Fuller, who got me to order the lifesaving blood test for the little girl having heart surgery. I've been moved by all the thousands of spirits who have come through to me over the years. I have learned from each of them. But these three stand out because of the strength of their energies and the transcendent power of their love. For some reason I cannot know, they have chosen to connect with me in a special way, teaching me important lessons. But even among this cherished group, Mikey is at the top.

Thus far in the story, Mikey probably seems like many other spirits you have read about in the preceding chapters: a child who died tragically and, through me, is reconnecting with his grieving and heartbroken family. And that's what he was to me at the point that his aunt came to me in the winter of 1994: A good, strong energy who came through clearly, but not a spirit who had distinguished itself from countless others. The reading was not one that stayed with me. (It is only recounted here with the aid of careful notes kept by Donna Kaplowitz).

Things began to change one night toward the end of 1994. I had a lucid dream—a visit—in which I went into my grandmother's bedroom and found a little boy sitting on her night table. He was about three years old, with sandy blond hair and big eyes. He was swinging his legs so that they banged on the night table. "Shhh," I told him. "You'll wake up Grandma."

My first thought was that he looked vaguely familiar; maybe he belonged to a distant cousin of mine. But I couldn't identify him further. I followed him into the closet, where my grandmother always kept Christmas presents.

"Who are you?" I asked.

He giggled and said, "I'm Mikey."

"Hi, Mikey," I said. "Who do you belong to?"

He didn't answer, just giggled again. And I woke up. The visit stayed with me for a few days, but I couldn't place the little boy. I knew it was significant if he was summoning the considerable energy it takes for a spirit to show itself in a visit. But I realized I would have to wait to find out who he was and why he had come to me.

Not long after, two women, a mother and her grown daughter, came to me for a reading. The older woman came in first, by herself. The strongest message that came through was not for her. It was for a female whose name sounded like "Shell." It came from the spirit of a little boy whose name began with "M." He said he wanted to talk to this "Shell" but that she was so nervous and upset that he was afraid he would hurt her more. Through the "M" and a few other details, the woman identified the spirit as that of her young grandchild, a boy named Michael. And she identified "Shell" as Michelle, her daughter and Michael's aunt. She was the young woman waiting downstairs. When she came upstairs, I told Michelle: "You need to calm down because there's someone who wants to talk to you but he's afraid he's going to hurt you more."

Michelle said she would try to relax and we proceeded. Michael came through with details of his death, saying he had drowned, and that Michelle was in the house, cooking, when it happened. It soon dawned on me that Michael was the "Mikey" who had come to me that night in my grandmother's room. And it would not be the last time he would drop by.

One night a few months before Sandra and I were married, I asked her to keep my new dog, Jolie, at her house for a night. Jolie was just a puppy, which is like having a baby in the house. I needed a good night's sleep and packed Jolie up for a night at Sandra's house.

Later that night I got into bed and began reading, propping my book up on my stomach. But I was soon interrupted by a visitor. Over the top of the book I saw the top of a little kid's head going by. I put the book down and looked for him. Nobody there. I put the book back up, and saw it again: the top of a little boy's head scampering by.

Then I heard a small child's voice say, "Where's the puppy?"

I knew instantly that it was Mikey; by now he had come through at enough readings that I recognized his vibration. For whatever reason, he was attaching himself to me.

"Mikey," I said, "the puppy's at Sandra's house. Concentrate on Sandra." I glanced at the clock and made a mental note that it was just past 11:00.

The next morning, I called Sandra. "So how was the dog last night?" I asked, silently wondering if she'd had a little visitor.

"Fine," Sandra said.

"Any accidents?"

"Only one."

"Where did she sleep?"

"She was in my bedroom with me."

"With you, on the bed?"

"Yes. Why, don't you think I can take care of the dog?" She was beginning to get annoyed, thinking I was quizzing her, which I was, though I didn't tell her why.

"Well, what was she doing around eleven o'clock?" I finally asked.

"I don't know."

"Sandra, just think. This is important to me."

"She was just nestled up next to me."

"That's it? The whole time?"

"Yes. Well, actually, around 11:15 she got up and went to the edge of the bed and started barking."

"What happened then?"

"Her tail wagged and then she came back and went back next to me. Why? What's going on?"

I told her about my little visit from Mikey and how I had sent him to her house. She was not amused. "Are you nuts?" she said. "You keep those people in your house. Don't send them here."

It was at our wedding, a few months later, that Mikey made his most dramatic appearance. At the reception, which was held at a country club, we were taking the traditional group pictures when it came time for us to be photographed with the ring bearer, my three-year-old cousin Nicky. He was being characteristically rambunctious, running around amid all the grown-up celebrating.

"Where's Nicky?" someone said. "We need him for the picture."

Just then, I felt a slight tug from down below, as if a small person was trying to get my attention. And I heard a child's voice say, with some urgency, "He's by the pool."

I took off, just about leaping down the staircase, and headed for the door to the pool. I saw that it was open. I went outside toward the pool but before I turned the corner that would give me a full view, I froze. For a moment I was afraid to look. My heart was pounding. When I turned the corner, I saw that Nicky was at the edge of the pool, bending over, about to go in. I scooped him up and brought him inside. His father began to cry. A few nights before he'd had a dream that Nicky drowned.

I have no doubt that it was Mikey who interceded. From the Other Side, he was using his own experience to help another three-year-old boy. It was his work. It was his gift to Nicky. And to me.

I was having many encounters with Mikey's family and he was showing up every time. I did a lecture in Florida, and he came through; it turned out another of his relatives was in the audience. It got to the point where I had to ask Mikey to come through in different ways because he was starting to feel like family—and I don't read my own family because I can't be objective. So I told him, "Listen, Mikey, you've come through so many times, and I know all about you and I know all about your family and I know how you passed. So you're going to have to start almost tricking me a little bit so I know it's really you and not my mind subconsciously thinking it's you."

Mikey complied with my request. One time, he came through with details fitting Mikey's life and death, but I didn't connect them to him because he told me his name was Robert. This was very clever. It turned out that when Mikey was born, his parents were undecided about a name. They had discussed naming him Michael, but Sally was reluctant because they had a nephew by the same name. They settled on Robert, but after the first day, decided it really didn't fit and went back to Michael. So for the first twenty-four hours of his life, Michael was Robert. And that's what he told me his name was throughout the reading, until he finally started showing me an "M."

In almost every reading I did for his family, Mikey made a point of mentioning something about "wrong sneakers." Explains Sally: "He had Barney sneakers he had grown out of. For the burial, I put his newer sneakers on him. But the Barney ones were his favorites."

And in the one reading when both Mikey's parents came together, he told me he wanted to thank them for displaying a particular picture. "You mean in the den, where we keep all his pictures?" Sally asked. No, I said. Mikey was showing me what looked like a cubby-hole, and next to it was a cup and also a key. They didn't recognize the description. But when they got home Sally was leaning on the counter in the kitchen, telling her sister Donna about the reading, when something caught her eye: part of the kitchen cabinetry was a group of Formica knickknack holders—cubbyholes. A loose picture of Mikey was in one of them. Next to that was a cup in which Sally kept loose change, and a keychain with Mikey's name on it.

Interestingly, when Sally came for her first reading, I thought her child was a girl. That was the way he came through. When she said he was a boy, I said, "Okay, but he's coming through very soft and sensitive. He's a mush." This word rang so true for his mother that she began to cry. "That's what I call him. He was my mush," she said. "Sometimes he would be just walking by you and he would grab your face and give you a kiss. He just had this mushy person-ality. So the fact that he came through that way is just astounding."

"He wants you to know you shouldn't blame yourself," I said. "He knows you've replayed it over and over again."

Sally said this was so true.

Then Mikey started telling me that among those who welcomed him to the Other Side was his great-grandfather.

"Oh, Mikey, you couldn't have had anyone better," Sally said.

Anthony, Mikey's dad, was the last member of the family to come for a reading. Though he was impressed, at times even amazed, by the information that had come through, he was the kind of person, said his wife, who you have to hit over the head with proof. "There were too many people going," Anthony remembers. "And I felt, let him rest in peace. Let it go. What can you tell me that's going to make me feel better?"

So why did he come? Curiosity, maybe. "I want to know but I don't want to know—that kind of thing," he says. But in his general skepticism about the process, he wanted to make sure that I didn't take advantage of the fact that I already knew so much. He made the appointment under a friend's name.

When he sat down and I asked to hold something personal, he handed me his wallet. (No, I didn't look inside.) I didn't know who was coming through but this spirit immediately gave me the feeling that he had waited a while for this. "The first thing I'm getting is that someone is here asking, 'What took you so long? I've been waiting.' "

Anthony smiled weakly.

"He says you don't believe in this, so to prove that he's really here he's telling me to tell you that it's okay to buy mom the dog."

I could tell it was on the mark. "I was devastated," Anthony said later. Before coming, he had taken his daughter, Cara, out for lunch and had discussed buying a dog for his wife.

Mikey then came through with his name, and I said to Anthony, "You're not connected to all the people who've been coming for Mikey, are you?" He said he was.

Now Mikey thanked his father for "finally" cleaning out his room; he said that by doing so he was moving things in the right direction. And he wanted his father to reassure his mother that his drowning wasn't her fault. Anthony says he felt "one hundred percent" that Mikey was there. "I didn't need to know any more," he said.

At one of the later readings for his family, Mikey said he was going to be very busy, that he might not come through for a while because he was going to do his "job," which he indicated was to help children pass over. This led Sally to decide that the family was coming for too many readings. "I believe that when they go over they still have work to do," she says. "And we can't just keep bothering him every time we get the urge."

I believe the reason Mikey chose to make such close connections with me is that there were so many issues of guilt and responsibility that needed to be addressed in his family that he felt the need to give them as much peace and closure as he could. I was the vehicle he used to assure them that they must not feel guilty and that he is still with them.

And because of the way he has shown that the cords of love are unbreakable, the experience has been profound for me as well. Mikey is not just another spirit to me. He is part of me now.

A nd so life in the physical world goes on, as it does in the spirit world. I hope that through this book I have given you a better understanding of how it is really all just one world.

Please know that in putting this book together, there were so many memories to pick from. I chose the events that I feel best exemplify my life and work—the experiences through which I have developed my philosophies about what spirit communication ultimately means. But in recounting my most memorable and compelling experiences, I realize I have probably also raised expectations. It is important to keep in mind that even the best mediums cannot maintain the highest level of communication at all times, yielding spectacular validating information every time they sit down to do a reading. This is not to say that an "average" reading is not positive. I believe that whether we receive one word of validation or enough to fill a book, it is important to acknowledge the enormous energy spirits are expending in order to come through. They are coming through for *us*—because they love us, and because they know the ultimate message is a vital one: In these modern, often cynical, times it is important to remember that we are all spiritual beings, and as such, we cannot die. We can only live and learn forever.

My goal in writing this book was not to convince you of anything. The real learning can only come as a result of your own personal experience. I hope I have answered many of your questions, dispelled some misconceptions, and eased some misgivings. There is still a lot I don't understand; a lot I hope to learn in the years to come. I can only hope that the experiences ahead are as profound and enlightening to me as those that I chronicled here, and that they continue to give me knowledge and understanding about the nature of our existence.

I hope I have given you enough to consider as you continue on your own journey. I might not have been able to give you a "One Last Time" through this book, but I hope the words do ring true, and that you take joy from their meaning.

REFERRALS

Lydia Clar
P.O. Box 300
263 Central Ave.
Jersey City, NJ 07307
(201) 223-6511

Starchild Books
Sandy Anastasi
3762 E. Rte. 41
Pt. Charlotte, FL 33952
(941) 743-0800

Shelley Peck
P.O. Box 604373
Bayside, NY 11360
(718) 279-0944

MaryJo McCabe
7914 Wrenwood Blvd.
Suite A
Baton Rouge, LA 70809
(504) 926-3355

Glenn Dove
P.O. Box 701
Baldwin, NY
(516) 223-2567

For further information on John Edward, his newsletter, seminars, and videos, you can write to him at:

John Edward
P.O. Box 383
Huntington, NY 11743

Or contact him at **www.johnedward.net**

ACCESS ENTERTAINMENT FOR DISCOUNT BENEFITS AND SERVICES is the proud sponsor of many of John Edward's events. If you would like more information regarding John Edward, web site events, videotapes, audiotapes, newsletter, and upcoming appearances around the country, or information about Access Entertainment, please fill out the following and mail it to the address below:

ACCESS ENTERTAINMENT
John Edward
P.O. Box 383
Huntington, NY 11743

(PLEASE PRINT)

Name   _____
Address   _____
City   _____
State   _____
Zip Code   _____
Phone   (D)_____(E)_____
E-Mail   _____